Praise for *Be Still*

"With this detailed study of the incident of Jesus calming the storm, Cherie Hill has not only brought new light to a familiar Gospel story, she has showed us how to both weather and grow from our personal storms. *Be Still* is a healing balm to the soul. My best advice — get this book, use it, and buy another one for your best friend!"
— Jim Thomson, M.A., LCPC, author and speaker.

"*Be Still* is a wealth of Scripture that readers can return to again and again for encouragement in the midst of trials. *Be Still* is not a book that you read once, put on your bookshelf, and then forget about. It's a book that doesn't promise quick fixes, or endless sunshine. Instead, it is a lifeline attached to God's Word, designed to help the reader find peace in the midst of each and every storm that comes their way."
— Deborah Porter, writer, editor, and radio talk show host.

"*Be Still — Let Jesus Calm Your Storms* combines intellectual common sense, Biblical Scriptures, and an author dedicated to helping people who have suffering in their lives. If you are currently going through a storm, this book can definitely help you through it. Buy a copy for yourself, buy a copy for a friend, or leave a copy somewhere for a stranger."
— Dan Blankenship, author of *The Running Girl.*

"The book nicely bridges the gap between those who doubt God because there are storms and the true lessons to be drawn from those storms. One of the best parts of this book is the way the author explores creating both inner and outer peace. Many people are more troubled in their minds than they are in reality; this book can help."
—Donald M. Mitchell, Amazon.com top 10 Reviewer, Harvard Graduate, author, and CEO featured in *Forbes Magazine.*

"*Be Still, Let Jesus Calm Your Storms,* by Cherie Hill, is an inspiring book that Christians, as well as all individuals who are seeking peace in a chaotic world, will find to be 'life-changing.' Regardless of where readers are in their walk with God, the words of the author and her use of Scripture to support her advice and encouragement will enable them to understand much more about faith and how it is the path that gives peace of mind in all situations."
—Bettie Corbin Tucker, IP reviewer, author and speaker.

"I can highly recommend this book to anyone who is looking for a fulfilling life purpose. Cherie Hill has a Bachelor of Arts in Psychology with a Certificate in Biblical Counseling, but her greatest accomplishment is making a difference in the lives of people who are in need of human caring, a few warm words of encouragement, and an open heart."
—Rebecca Johnson, Amazon.com top 10 Reviewer.

BE STILL

Let Jesus Calm Your Storms

Cherie Hill

This book is dedicated to God . . .
the *perfect author* of my life.
My greatest joy is just in "knowing" You.
Thank you for teaching me to "*Be Still.*"
Most of all, thank you for loving me enough
to use my life according to *Your* purposes.

CONTENTS

PREFACE

I would like to take a moment to explain exactly how this book was inspired and why I believe it can deeply change your life.

As a born again Christian, I began asking God to give my life purpose and fill me in a way that the world could not. I needed something that was eternal and meaningful. And well, God answered me. I believe that God has always had a plan for me, yet it was only when I finally reached out to Him that He revealed His purpose for my life. God began to show me all of the "spiritual gifts" that He had given to me. He gave me insight as to how all of my life experiences had strengthened and developed those gifts.

You see, I have always been a good listener. For some reason, people have always felt more than comfortable revealing their most intimate problems in their lives to me. I never understood why complete strangers would open up and express their deepest pains and "storms" of life, while looking to me for some type of answer. Many times, I found myself overwhelmed with empathy, yet filled with sorrow because I was unable to provide answers or even point them in the right direction. When God finally revealed His plan for my life, I began to see the whole picture come together. God had a vision for my life . . . and it was in my moment of surrender that He gave me eyes to see.

God began to teach me how critical Scripture is to our lives; His Word has become the very breath that gives me life. His plan for me was to lead others to Jesus by simply providing them with Scriptures that would speak directly to their circumstances. It is in receiving God's grace that we can live with confident hope—it is His Word that gives us the faith we need to receive that grace. It really is the Truth that sets us free and fills us with hope. His Word produces a faith in us that will never fail.

And so, to make a long story short, God revealed "ScriptureNow.com" to me. I can honestly tell you that it has been the greatest blessing in my life and in the lives of hundreds of thousands of people in over 30 countries around the world. I can't imagine one day of my life going by without reaching out and sharing the Word of God to people in this way! And God did all of this in the midst of my raging storms of life.

This is where "Be Still" took on its purpose . . . as I have read the countless prayer requests through ScriptureNow.com, God spoke to me and showed me the miracle of "Jesus Calms the Storm" in a whole new light. This miracle goes to the heart of every single situation that we face in life, and I believe God filled me with the wisdom and insight to be able to write this book for *you*.

I hope that this book touches your heart and speaks to you through its message. I pray that you will always draw close to God, so that He can comfort, encourage, and rescue you through all of life's storms. I pray that you will also visit me at **http://www.ScriptureNow.com** and experience a great blessing in your life!

Testimonies from ScriptureNow.com

I 'm wondering if this is really God's email…
the Scriptures you send speak so directly to me…
that it must be.

Oh, what a blessing . . . I am so thankful to God that I found your website. God speaks to me through you.

Thank you for your Scriptures, they seem to always come on time.

Thank you! It's amazing how the Scriptures have gone in line with what I am dealing with!!

Thank you so much for your never ending help in my life. The Scriptures were helpful, powerful, and effective in my life.

You have helped save my life. My crisis is over and God gave me a miracle!

God bless you mightily for your compassionate ministry.

I don't know how you knew, but this Scripture was exactly what I needed. Thank you!!!

Thank you. This is what I needed to hear!

I had lost all hope until I found your website, and now I am filled with a hope I have never felt before.

Thank you for all of your prayers and love over this year and for being a safe place to call out to. I can't tell you just how much the daily Scriptures have blessed my heart.

You know, before I found out about ScriptureNow.com, I was not lost, but not headed in the right direction.

I will never be able to express the power I have experienced in the Scriptures that you send.

You will never fully understand how God has used your website to turn my life around and get me moving in the right direction.

The nine Scriptures that you sent have given me nine days of strength. I had never experienced God speaking to me until now. Thank you for using His Word to help me hear Him.

Thank you from the bottom of my heart for your prayers and your concerns. I don't think I could have coped with the pressures I have found myself under if it would not have been for your caring and sending me Scripture and prayer. I now know that I will overcome through Christ!

I look so forward to receiving your Daily Scripture. It just seems as though God is speaking right through it!

You will never quite understand the impact your Ministry is having.

May God richly bless you for the work you are doing for Him.

INTRODUCTION

The Storm

Do you feel as though you're in a raging storm? Storms of life flood your spirit with disillusionment, despair, and disappointment. The consuming waves of a storm in life can submerge your soul with agonizing fear. When you're in a storm of life, it feels as though each breath might be your last. The ongoing destruction from the storm forces you to cling to anything and everything, in the hopes of somehow surviving it all. As the storm continues to rage, you suddenly realize that there's no lifeboat—there's no quick escape. You're on your own. Usually, very quickly, the terror sets in; with it comes despair and hopelessness. The desperation that overcomes you, suddenly, becomes more than you can withstand. As the end seems to be drawing nearer, with each moment that passes, all you can do is stand by and watch it all unfold.

Our storms of life bring us to the point where we realize that we have nowhere to go, but to God. In a moment of overwhelming desperation, when we finally do call out to Him, we suddenly realize that our relationship with Him has grown cold. Through our cries for help, without stable ground to stand on, it's anger that takes over and we shout,

"Lord, don't you care?"

We've all been there, at one time or another. If you haven't experienced a storm in your life, then praise God; but, get ready because Jesus assured us:

"I have told you all this so
that you may have peace in me.
Here on earth you will have many trials and sorrows.
But take heart, because I have overcome the world."
(John 16:33 NLT)

The Controversy of the Miracle

The miracle of "Jesus Calms the Storm" has been called one of the most controversial miracles that Jesus performed. Even today, we witness those who are pronounced dead . . . receive life again, blind who against all odds see, illnesses that are cured without explanation, and tragic accidents where miraculously people survive. We witness miracles every day and realize that they are from the power of something far greater than what we can comprehend.

Yet, even in the face of such miracles, we allow human reasoning to get the best of us. Doubt, more often than not, wins out. We end up walking by sight, instead of by faith. So, we wrestle with our faith, just as the Disciples did on the Sea of Galilee. The battle begins . . . *within.* How do we accept someone controlling the wind and the waves in a violent storm? Even if we want to believe, this kind of miracle pushes our faith a little farther than we'd like. This kind of faith shoves us outside of our comfort zone.

We like to keep God in a box. We're comfortable with Him in some things in our lives, but not others. We're content in keeping Him where we've put Him . . . allowing Him out of the box is just too risky — we're not sure what to expect from Him. We're not convinced He'll do things the *way* they should be done or in the *timing* that they should be done. We believe that it's possible for Him to heal someone we're praying for, but we're just not certain that He can do anything in *our* situation. We're convinced that there are just some things that God is either too busy to deal with, or He just really doesn't care. It has been said that to ask God for help in "small things" is wasting His time — be assured, *ALL things are small to God.* He is looking to and fro the earth for someone to not only call out to Him, but to *believe Him* (2 Chronicles 16:9).

He is looking for *your* faith *in the midst of your storms of life.* He has allowed the storm, in an effort to increase your faith, *by threatening to destroy it.* Out of His great love for you, He calls out to you through your storm and asks, *"Who do you say I am"* (Matthew 16:15)?

As your life is pushed to the edge, His voice calls down from heaven . . . demanding an answer. It is your answer that determines whether or not you will make it through the storm and if there will be anything left in the aftermath.

This miracle is for you to understand the purpose of the storms in your life and how to persevere through them. By applying this miracle to your life, you will find that God can calm all of your storms . . . if you will just have faith that He can.

It is your faith in God that makes *all* the difference. Trust Him, and cling to your faith . . .

God ALWAYS keeps His Word.

*According to your faith
and trust and reliance
[on the power invested in Me]
be it done to you;*
(Matthew 9:29 AMP)

The miracle in the storm on the Sea of Galilee revealed the Disciples' lack of faith in Jesus as the Son of God. Although they had witnessed Jesus perform many miracles, they still had doubt about who He really was. It was through this miracle that their faith was truly put to the test. The Disciples believed, just as most people did, that many miracles are understandably possible, *but only God* could control the wind and the waves. There was no doubt in their minds that this kind of power could only come from the hand of God. God's desire is to move His hand in your storms as well. *He is looking for your faith.*

What you must understand is that this miracle was not just a story of God's awesome power — it was not just another miracle. This miracle was for *you* to understand the purpose of the storms in *your* life and how to persevere through them. By applying this miracle to your life, you will find that God can calm all of your storms . . . *if you will just have faith that He can.*

Storms Will Come

After receiving thousands of emails from people all over the world through the ScriptureNow.com Ministry, I might guess that your storms are a broken relationship, a shattered marriage, depression, despair over unsaved loved ones, job anxiety, unemployment, financial failure, an illness, death, or some unexpected tragedy. Maybe you feel that life in general is a raging storm. No matter how big or small your storm, you feel that no one seems to understand; you're convinced that you're in the boat alone. With each agonizing moment that passes, you feel that you're one day closer to drowning; it seems as though nothing and no one can save you.

If you aren't currently in a storm, be on the lookout. The enemy is looking for an opportunity to send the perfect storm into your life. He is well aware of our deepest desires and our innermost struggles. Satan not only attacks us where we are weakest; more often, he attacks in those areas where we feel we are strongest. He knows exactly where pride exists. He knows we won't see an attack coming when we're overly confident in a particular area of our lives. He knows those places in our lives where we've decided to play God and we've shut God out. He's able to see any crack we leave in the doorway, and He feels more than comfortable letting himself in. The enemy is always at work, and he is more than willing to kick you while you're down. He's not particularly concerned about what's going on in your life and whether or not the timing is convenient. He's simply out to destroy your faith in God. The enemy's attacks are deceitful and destructive—you won't even see what's coming. Just as in the miracle of Jesus Calms the Storm, many times, the storms of our lives will come from out of nowhere—unexpectedly.

> *God knew your storm was coming,*
> *trust Him to take you through it.*

How many times have we judged others and said, "I'd never do that. That could never happen to me ... I'm too loving, too giving, too faithful, too loyal, too obedient, too prayerful, too dedicated to God. Besides, I go to church on Sunday!" Before we know it, we find ourselves in the midst of that *very* storm; we're dazed and confused, wondering how we got there and how to get out.

The Storm Has Great Purpose

The Disciples were not exempt from a test of faith and neither are we. God's purposes for them were so great, so critical to His plans, that He allowed a raging storm to take over their boat on the Sea of Galilee — bringing them to the edge of their faith. He increased their faith by asking them to step into a boat and *risk it*.

Faith isn't faith, unless it requires taking a step into the unseen. It doesn't take faith at all to cling to what you see. The faith that God is after is a faith that clings to Him and isn't threatened or destroyed by adversity and uncertainty.

You know that you have genuine faith when common sense tells you to stop believing, but you continue to trust God anyway. *It's all about your faith in God* — don't ever believe otherwise.

This unexpected storm tested these men, who considered themselves *very* skilled fishermen, so that their faith would be strengthened for the journey ahead. In their weakness, they realized they were helpless without their Savior. When Jesus performed the incredible miracle of calming the storm, it caused these expert fishermen, who had been through many storms on this Sea, to experience a storm that would bring them to the end of themselves. Although the Disciples were master fishermen, God took the area of the Disciples' lives where they felt most confident . . . and tested them. God knew they needed to be brought to the end of their own abilities, so that they would trust in His.

Faith isn't faith,
unless it believes in the unseen.
It doesn't take faith at all
to cling to what you see.
Faith in God trusts Him even
when you can't see the very
next step in front of you.

Rest assured, God is bringing you to your knees, so that you can witness His hand lift you up. The message that God needed the Disciples to understand was that it was *by faith alone* that they could be saved. It's the message He wants *you* to know, as well.

But people are declared righteous
because of their faith,
not because of their work.
(Romans 4:5 NLT)

By sending the storm and testing them in it, God turned these men into the greatest witnesses for Christ that the world has ever known. *Our* storms will also come in those areas where we least expect them. Our pride will keep us from seeing the storms coming. It is in the areas where pride exists that Satan sees an easy target. Don't be deceived . . . God *allowed* the storm in this miracle, and He's allowing it in your life . . . with a plan to use it ALL for *your good* and His glory!

Then the Lord asked Satan, 'Have you noticed my servant Job? He is the finest man in all the earth — a man of complete integrity. He fears God and will have nothing to do with evil.' Satan replied to the Lord, 'Yes, Job fears God, but not without good reason! You have always protected him and his home and his property from harm. You have made him prosperous in everything he does. Look how rich he is! But take away everything he has, and he will surely curse you to your face!' 'Alright, you may test him,' the Lord said to Satan. 'Do whatever you want with everything he possesses, but don't harm him physically.' So Satan left the Lord's presence. (Job 1:8-12 NLT)

Never doubt that there are spiritual conversations about *you*. Yes, *you*! You are known by name in the heavenly realms, and we know this from Isaiah 45:3 (NLT):

I am the Lord, the God of Israel,
the one who calls you by name.

You are no different than Job or the Disciples; in that, God will only allow those things which He knows will bring you closer to Him, give Him the glory, and make your heart more like His. It is imperative to truly understand that God will never give you more than you can withstand, and He will always make a way through your storms when you trust in Him.

But remember that the temptations
that come into your life are no different
from what others experience.
And God is faithful.
He will keep the temptation
from becoming so strong
that you can't stand up against it.
When you are tempted,
he will show you a way out
so that you will not give into it.
(1 Corinthians 10:13 NLT)

When you feel that God has allowed your storms, you should be comforted in just knowing that God alone is control of them. In your storms of life, your spirit can be quieted by grabbing hold of the Truth: If God has allowed a storm . . .

He will make a way through it.

He has assured you that He is with you *always* (Matthew 28:20). You should feel secure, in just knowing, that God has set the boundaries and perimeters of your storm—just as he did with Job. It should strengthen you to know that God is allowing this storm only because He knows the blessing behind it.

When God is at work in your life, you will often experience the miraculous and sufficient power of God in your storms . . . *even more than in your times of great blessings.*

We can only truly appreciate the glory of being on the mountaintop when we've had to climb up from the valley. And the only way from one mountaintop to the next is *through* the valleys. It's in the valley where the richest soil in the world is found . . . *God knows what He's doing when He's growing your faith.*

It is only through the storms that you will truly know the heart of God. In your storms, you've been given the opportunity to encounter God—the choice to accept His invitation is yours.

As long as we insist on being in control, God will not interfere. He will allow us to go our own way, until we come to a place of surrender. In order to experience God's miracles in our lives, we must be willing to relinquish control, and *let God be God.*

> *If God has allowed the storm,*
> *He will make a way through it.*
> *Be certain that God is only allowing*
> *the storm because He knows the*
> *blessing behind it. Through the storm,*
> *God is giving you the opportunity*
> *to experience, first hand,*
> *His miraculous and*
> *sufficient power in your life.*

Too often, instead of trusting in God's sovereign purpose in our storms, many of us feel anger. We feel like God allowed us to walk into the storm or that He even led us right into it. We're convinced that He could have spared us the pain and suffering. Understanding the purpose of your storms will help you persevere through them and bring you closer to God, instead of casting your soul deeper into despair by allowing your heart to become hardened in your distress.

In all this, Job did not sin by blaming God.
(Job 1:22 NLT)

(If you have not read the book of Job . . . I challenge you to do so and understand what it truly means to have faith in God through the most tragic storms of life.)

Why A Storm?

We live in a world filled with anxiety and tremendous uncertainty. Each and every day we are confronted by stories that shake the foundation of our faith — to a point of near destruction. If we, personally, aren't facing unthinkable trials and tragedies, we worry about friends and family members who are facing the inconceivable. Or we become fearful of what *lies ahead* in our lives.

We wonder what *good* could possibly come from such overwhelming anxiety and fear. But, it's in the worst of times that we find the most opportune moment to re-examine our lives. What have we taken for granted? What are our morals and values? On what have we built our foundation and will it be able to withstand the storms in our lives? In the storms of life, we have two choices: we can reaffirm the faith we embraced when we accepted Christ into our life, or we can walk away. For those who have never known Jesus, these times of suffering are an opportunity for the heart to be opened and the need for God to surface. God is at work, even when we are unaware. The storms convince us that we're lost and in need of help. In our desperation, we realize that we need a "compass."

When you're holding a compass, you can turn your feet in any direction, but the arrow of the compass will faithfully point to Magnetic North. If you should ever become lost, the compass will give you an indication of where you are and where you're going. In life, "North" is Christ. We may take a path that leads us in the "world's" direction and we might get lost along the way; but, when we turn to Christ, He realigns our lives in the direction of God's will. Jesus performs many miracles in our storms of life— showing us that He is all that we need, when there is a need, is just one of them.

> *Jesus performs many miracles*
> *in our storms of life —*
> *showing us that He is ALL we need,*
> *when there is a need, is just one of them.*

Whether you're a person of faith in God, or a person still questioning and seeking answers, it's likely that you're open-minded to miracles. If you don't need a miracle right now, you probably know someone who does.

You see, God does extraordinary things for ordinary people. He loves to surprise us with His goodness and His power, in order to help us in our most desperate times. He can do anything. But, in the storms of your life, He wants you to know His presence, so that as you wait for His perfect timing, you can be filled with hope. He wants you to find security and peace in His care; He wants you trusting that He is mighty to save (Zephaniah 3:17).

> *God wants to give you a miracle in your storm, but it's less about the actual miracle and more about your personal encounter with Him.*
> *He wants to give you a persevering faith that will see you through the journey.*

If you want to find an extraordinary miracle in the life of an ordinary man, you need to look no further than to Moses. Moses was traveling in the desert when God spoke to him through a burning bush. (If you want to get an amazing glimpse of God's awesome power, you should make it a priority to read through the book of Exodus.) God caught Moses off-guard, in the middle of the desert, through a burning bush. His encounter with God was life–altering. This miracle enabled Moses to walk forward in faith, trusting God, because he could not deny such a supernatural occurrence. Moses was able to walk through even greater adversity along his journey because with each step of faith that he took . . . God strengthened his faith through one miracle after another.

God used a burning bush to initially get Moses' *attention;* then, when Moses came to examine the bush further, *God called out his name.* (In our storms of life . . . God calls out our name, too. He wants our undivided attention.)

As Moses drew even closer to God, God stopped him and told him to take off his shoes because he was standing on holy ground. He wanted Moses to know that he was in the presence of Almighty God. He wanted him to remember that moment *forever.* That event is now remembered thousands of years later — God's miracle made its mark on history.

> *Our storms come with an objective*
> *that is far more significant than*
> *our present need for comfort.*
> *God is doing us a favor, by bringing us to*
> *a place of forfeiting our will in our lives,*
> *so that we will embrace His.*

In this particular miracle, God didn't stop with a burning bush. He goes on to tell Moses that He has heard the cries of His people in their suffering, and He has come down to save them. In your storms of life, God wants to step in and give you a miracle, too. But, it's less about the actual miracle and more about your encounter with Him. He wants to give you the faith that will see you through the storms of your life that are yet to come. *And they will come.*

The poet Elizabeth Barrett Browning once famously wrote that *"Earth is crammed full of heaven, and every common bush aglow with God. Those who see . . . take off their shoes."* God wants to bring *you* to a place of "taking off *your* shoes."

This miracle on the Sea of Galilee, this storm, was preparing the Disciples' faith for the journey ahead. It was the storm that would bring them to their knees and really get their attention. God also knows exactly what storms you and I will need to go through, in order to draw us closer to Him:

> *Our storms come with an objective*
> *that is far more significant*
> *than our present need for comfort.*

God is doing us a favor by bringing us to a place of forfeiting all of our expectations in our lives, so that we will embrace His. Your storms can create the greatest intimacy between yourself and God. There is *nothing* more awesome. When you're walking with God, the emptiness and loneliness that daily consumes your soul is filled with a joy that overflows and a peace that is beyond all understanding.

This miracle was not just for the Disciples — it was for *you*. You will experience a miracle in your life, if you will understand how significant the storms of your life are to your faith. You must realize that God can do ANYTHING — He *can* calm the storm. But, what He really wants to do is use your life for His purposes—something far greater than anything you could dare ask for or imagine (Ephesians 3:20). He wants to give you something far more fulfilling than you could ever desire.

It should be encouraging to know that if God could take these few ordinary men and use this storm to change the world forever through their testimony . . . *He can use your storms for His glory, too.*

Yes, God wants to use *you.* Rest assured He can perform miracles in your life, in your storms, just as He did when He calmed the Sea of Galilee. The question is, **"Do *you* believe He can?"**

Then Jesus told him,
"You believe because you have seen me.
Blessed are those who haven't seen me
and believe anyway."
(John 20:29 NLT)

"What do you mean, 'If I can'?" Jesus asked.
"Anything is possible if a person believes."
(Mark 9:23 NLT)

God intends to perform a miracle in your life and not have you say, *"How did He do that?"* Instead, He wants for you to have the same experience as the Disciples of Jesus had—it was in their awe and amazement that they asked, *"Who is this man, that even the winds and waves obey him?"*

And they were filled with awe amazement.
They said to one another 'Who is this man,
that even the winds and waves obey him?'
(Luke 8:25 NLT)

God desires for you to be in such awe and amazement of His power that you are less concerned about how He did it, but rather, *who* it is that did it! We beg and beg for miracles in our lives, constantly wondering why God won't do something; yet, when He does, He mystifies us even more. It's our heart He's after, and He's more than willing to bring about a miracle in your life in order to capture it. His miracle for you is that you will not be overcome by your storms, but that you will know Who to come to when your storms emerge. He's strengthening your faith in Him *through* the storms. He wants us to get the message loud and clear: Our faith is not strengthened by striving after it, but by resting in Him, *the Faithful One.*

God is strengthening our faith
in the storms of our lives, and He wants us
to get the message loud and clear —
our faith is not strengthened by striving
after it, but by resting in Him,
the Faithful One.

Just as in the Sea of Galilee, God knows our storms often come from out of nowhere. He's well aware that when they do . . . we're likely to go into shear panic. His miracle for you, in the storm, is that you can be at rest with Him through your faith.

> *God knows what He's doing.*
> *Let the storms come,*
> *and let the waters rise —*
> *God is taking you deeper.*

We look at the storms of our lives and too often, ask, *"If God is so loving, why does He allow pain and suffering in my life? What have I done to deserve being a victim in this circumstance? Why do I need to go through this storm? Why can't He just take me around it? I want out and NOW!"* The truth is, God knows us . . . He knows what it will take to bring us to our knees. It is upon our knees where we learn to walk by faith and receive the peace that only He can provide when storms arise.

Remember this clearly:
ANYTHING that drops us to our knees
and brings us to the foot of the Cross
is GOOD for us.

In our moments of complete brokenness, when the flesh is weak, but the spirit is willing (Matthew 26:41), He wants us to know: *In Jesus* we will find confident patience, strength, endurance, and peace.

God knows exactly what we need, in order to make it through this journey of life. At times, our journey will take us into unfamiliar, intimidating, territory . . . which may be exactly where God wants us, so that He can perform His greatest work in our lives.

> *God wants you in the back*
> *of the boat with Jesus —*
> *a place of peace and rest.*
> *He wants you to "Be Still";*
> *yet, we find that "being still"*
> *requires action . . . it demands our faith.*

If we go back to the book of Exodus, and the life of Moses, we find that when Pharaoh finally let the people go, God did not lead them along the main road that ran through the territory — *even though that was the shortest route to the Promised Land.* Here's what He said, *'If the people are faced with a battle, they might change their minds and return to Egypt.' So God led them in a round-about way through the wilderness toward the Red Sea* (Exodus 13:17-18 NLT). You see, God may have led them the long way, but He was preparing an even greater miracle than Him *rescuing* them.

You might be tempted to believe that God doesn't know what He's doing—that He's causing you to endure unnecessary pain and suffering—but, rest assured, God knows exactly what He's doing. Let the storms come, and let the waters rise—*God is taking you deeper*.

God knows that this won't be the last storm you will encounter in your life. It's a fallen world; He wants to build your faith in Him, so when the seas rage and the storm clouds begin closing in . . . you will find peace **in Him**.

> *Don't worry about anything;*
> *instead pray about everything.*
> *Tell God what you need, and thank him for all he has done.*
> *If you do this, you will experience God's peace, which is far*
> *more wonderful than the human mind can understand.*
> *His peace will guard your hearts and minds*
> *as you live in Christ Jesus.*
> (Philippians 4:6-7 NLT)

Faith Can Calm the Storm

Through God's Word, we are assured that He can calm the "external" storm; but, the storm He really wants to calm is the one *inside* of you—the "internal" storm. Ask yourself, while reading through this miracle, "Was Jesus just simply telling the wind and the waves, *'Peace! Be Still!'*? Or was there a deeper message?" Jesus was speaking to YOU in this miracle. You see, it took no effort at all for Jesus to calm the external, physical storm. It was much more important for Him to teach us how to calm the storm within us — the "spiritual" storm. When you learn how to calm the storm within, through your faith in God, the wind and the waves may be threatening to take you under, but you will find yourself in the eye of the storm . . . *at peace*.

We can look at a hurricane as being symbolic to our storms of life. Hurricanes have a distinctive feature called an "eye." The eye of a hurricane is in the middle of the spiral of the storm. The eye is produced by the spiraling action of the storm, and it is the area where the air is slowly sinking. When the eye of a hurricane passes over an area, the winds decrease to a gentle breeze and the rain stops. In the eye of the hurricane, you may even be able to see the sun during the day or the stars out at night. Then, as the rest of the storm passes and the wind suddenly changes directions, the storm becomes ferocious again.

God wants you to be in the eye of your storms in life. In the eye, He knows that you will be able to see the light of day and enjoy the beauty of the stars at night. In the eye of storm, the winds and waters may rage around you, but you will be experiencing peace in the midst of it. God has given us His Word, the Scriptures, to keep us from being overcome by the most powerful winds that reside just outside the eye wall of the storm.

Understanding the miracle of "Jesus Calms the Storm" makes us certain of one thing: Whatever the storm is, however fierce, and however the storm came about, God can calm it. The question is, "Will *you* have faith that God can calm *your* storm?" The lesson in this fantastic miracle of "*Jesus Calms the Storm*" is to have confident faith in God and get to the back of the boat with Jesus — a place of peace and rest. What we also learn through this miracle is that "*Being Still,*" actually, requires action. Let the miracle of Jesus calming the storm increase your faith and bring about a miracle in *your life,* by teaching you to...

"Be Still"

NOTE TO READER: *I encourage you to go through this book and highlight the Scriptures. When you only have a moment, skim through the book and be encouraged!*

Also, don't miss the section in the back of this book, "God's Word On . . ." Use the section as a reference to God's Promises that will encourage your faith through all your storms of life.

Chapter 1

⚓ Understanding the Storm ⚓

Jesus Calms the Storm

On that day, when evening had come, he said to them, "Let us go across to the other side." And leaving the crowd, they took him with them in the boat, just as he was. And other boats were with him. And a great windstorm arose, and the waves were breaking into the boat, so that the boat was already filling. But he was in the stern, asleep on the cushion. And they woke him and said to him, "Teacher, do you not care that we are perishing?" And he awoke and rebuked the wind and said to the sea, "Peace! Be Still!" And the wind ceased, and there was a great calm. He said to them, "Why are you so afraid? Have you still no faith? (Mark 4:35-40 ESV)*

Then Jesus asked, "Where is your faith?" And they were filled with awe and amazement. They said to one another, "Who is this man, that even the winds and waves obey him?"(Luke 8:25 NLT)

In order to understand the miracle of "Jesus Calms the Storm," we must first understand the power of the sea; what its power represented then and now.

According to the Gospels, Jesus' ministry was centered around the Sea of Galilee. While many important events occurred in Jerusalem, Jesus spent most of His ministry along the shore of this freshwater lake. It was there that Jesus gave more than half of His parables and where He performed most of His miracles.

The Sea of Galilee was known for its sudden, violent storms. When it raged, the threat of drowning among fisherman was all too real. The Sea of Galilee is unique in that it is seven hundred feet below sea level, making it the lowest freshwater lake on the earth. At its widest point, the lake measures thirteen miles from north to south and seven and a half miles from east to west. Its deepest point is estimated at around two hundred feet.

The Sea's location was significant because it made the Sea susceptible to the sudden and violent storms. The storms would often develop when an east wind dropped cool air over the warm air rising from the Sea. This change produced well known furious storms, *without warning.*

The word "sea," in Hebrew, comes from the name of the evil god in the Babylonian creation story. It meant "evil" and "a mysterious and threatening force opposed to God." When Hebrews wanted to declare God's authority, they spoke of His power over the sea. In Psalms 89:9 (NKJV), the Psalmist said,

> *You rule the raging of the sea,*
> *when its waves rise, you still them.*

In Psalm 107:23-30 (NLT), we not only find a prophecy of "Jesus Calms the Storm," but an acknowledgement of God's power over the storms.

Some went off in ships, plying the trade routes of the world. They too, observed the Lord's power in action, his impressive works on the deepest seas. He spoke, and the winds rose, stirring up the waves. Their ships were tossed to the heavens and sank again to the depths; the sailors cringed in terror. They reeled and staggered like drunkards and were at wits' end. "Lord, help!" they cried in their trouble, and he saved them from their distress. He calmed the storm to a whisper and stilled the waves. What a blessing was that stillness as he brought them safely into the harbor!

As powerful as storms were and still are today, God is acknowledged to have power over them all. Never forget this truth in your own life: *God is in control.* The question is, "When a storm arises, will you cry out to the *One* who can help you?"

It was known that storms on this Sea could arise from nowhere; so, since Jesus was the Son of God, one might think that *surely* He knew there would be a great storm on this venture across the Sea. And if this were so, why did He choose to take His Disciples into it? You would almost expect, since Jesus was with the Disciples on this trip across the Sea, they would be free from worry. We can be certain they didn't expect to encounter a raging storm that they may have experienced on many other trips.

> *Never forget that God is in control.*
> *The question is,*
> *"When a storm arises,*
> *will you cry out to the*
> *only One who can help you?"*

Certainly, the Disciples who gave up everything in life and obediently followed Jesus would be protected from harm's way. They might even expect that this would be the most wonderful venture across the Sea that they had ever experienced. They more than likely found confidence in their commitment to Jesus and felt secure in His ability to protect them. They loved Jesus, believed in Him, and left behind everything in life to follow Him; yet, the Disciples' devotion did nothing to protect them from the terror of this storm.

In the Boat

Many times, we as Christians feel the same way the Disciples did . . . when we become a Christian and accept Jesus as Lord and Savior, shouldn't we be protected? We, understandably, *assume* that life should be "easier"; we feel certain that we should instantly have a closer relationship with God. We can falsely believe that we no longer have to endure "storms" in our lives. But, then, suddenly, one day, in one moment in time, we're faced with the painful truth—*it's not the way it works.* Our false expectations can create a storm in and of itself. When life doesn't happen just as we think it should, the winds start roaring and the storm clouds look ferocious. Our faith can begin to fail amidst the overwhelming atmosphere of doubt and despair.

> *Jesus didn't come to get you out of*
> *the storms in your life —*
> *He came to take you through them.*

When we make a stand in our faith, when we decide to get into the boat with Jesus, Satan unleashes his rage against us. We are now "officially" his enemy, and the true battle has begun. Shockingly, as we take each step of faith, our storms seem to actually come *more often* than *before* we believed!

When we're faced with the storms that we must endure, when walking with God, we find ourselves in the midst of our storm crying out, *"Why is this happening to me? If You're a God of love, why all this pain? Why do the innocent suffer? If You're a God of order, why all the chaos? If You're so powerful, why do You seem so incapable? By the way, where are You?"* It is at this time that we need to be reminded of the Truth—Jesus told us in John 16:33 (NLT):

> *"I have told you all this*
> *so that you may have peace in me.*
> *Here on earth you will have*
> *many trials and sorrows.*
> *But take heart, because I have overcome the world."*

When you're in the boat with Jesus, the answers to your questions come in many *unexpected* ways. *Sometimes,* they come by way of a storm that threatens to take you under.

> *In the storms of your life, God is always at work —*
> *drawing you closer to Him and weaving all*
> *of your paths into His purposes.*

You see, instead of presenting just an "ordinary" trial with an "ordinary storm," the storm in this miracle would be like no other. This storm would threaten to take the Disciples' very lives. This storm would ultimately test their faith. This miracle would cause the Disciples to ask, "*Who is this man?*"

It's interesting that the most violent storm these fishermen had ever experienced was when Jesus, the Son of God, was in the boat with them. It should be comforting to know that in the most violent storms of your life . . . *Jesus is in the boat with you, too.*

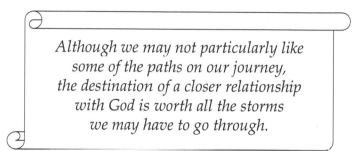

Although we may not particularly like some of the paths on our journey, the destination of a closer relationship with God is worth all the storms we may have to go through.

Understanding the storms of your life is realizing that although the waves may start crashing in on you . . . *Jesus is with you.* More importantly, you must be assured through His Word: He will not allow you to perish, if you will acknowledge His presence in your life and call out His name. Surely, your boat cannot go down with the Son of God in it! Don't be deceived, Jesus didn't come to get you out of the storms in your life—He came to take you *through* them.

You see, God knew that the Disciples needed to go from "here" to "there," in order to experience the miracle. He needed to take them from "here" to "there" **in their faith**—it's no different in our own lives.

God wants to take us from "here," in our faith, and bring us "there" — a place of walking in greater faith for the journey ahead.

When you take a journey with Jesus, it's like nothing you've ever experienced. It's simply not of this world. When you're walking with Jesus, you're taking a supernatural, spiritual, journey where He prepares you to live eternally.

Although we may not particularly like some of the paths on our journey . . . the destination of a closer relationship with God is worth all the storms we may have to endure. If you're following Jesus, you know where you're going — He's assured you of the destination. It's all about the journey getting there. He'll take you step by step because *He doesn't want you to miss a thing.*

I have refined you but not in the way silver is refined.
Rather, I have refined you
in the furnace of suffering.
I will rescue you for my sake—
yes, for my own sake!
(Isaiah 48:10 NLT)

It is often asked, "Was this the miracle of God calming the storm in the Sea or the miracle of Jesus teaching us how to calm the storm inside of us?" Jesus knew His Disciples' hearts, just like He knows your heart and mine.

O Lord, you have examined my heart
and know everything about me.
You know when I sit down or stand up.
You know my every thought when far away.
You chart the path ahead of me and tell me where to stop
and rest. Every moment you know where I am.
You know what I am going to say
even before I say it, Lord.
You both precede and follow me.
You place your hand of blessing on my head.
(Psalm 139:2 NLT)

As God lovingly allows us to venture into the storms of our lives, He is always at work—drawing us closer and closer to Him while weaving all our paths into His purposes. If you're trusting in God, you can't just look at your circumstances and think

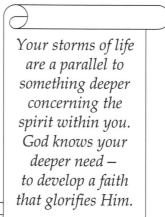

Your storms of life are a parallel to something deeper concerning the spirit within you. God knows your deeper need — to develop a faith that glorifies Him.

that is all there is to it. They are a parallel to something deeper and more important concerning the spirit within you.

In the storms of our lives, God will show us that we have a deeper need. We need to develop the faith that glorifies Him. We must recognize that we are in the hands of a loving Father who has put us right where we need to be, in order to teach us His ways and His will.

The answers for the storms in our lives come through the still small voice of God saying, *"I will not let you go down. You have no reason to despair. Rest in My Word. I am with you always."*

Through His Word, He assures us that He has everything under control, and there is no reason to fear. In the words of an old Hymn:

> *Day by day and with each passing moment,*
> *Strength I find to meet my trials here;*
> *Trusting in my Father's wise bestowment,*
> *I've no cause for worry or for fear.*

If we want to understand God's purpose in the storm, we must learn that God has allowed the storms in our lives out of love and wisdom. God designed life to be full of the unexpected, so that we will constantly be reminded that *we're not in control.*

Satan fills us with the lies that we are our own gods, we are in charge, we can plan, and we can direct our future; to the degree that God has given us free will . . . there is some truth to that. But, the devil distorts it and leads us to believe that we can control *everything*. As hard as we might try . . . *we can't.* Jesus himself reminded us,

> *"I tell you the truth,*
> *the Son can do nothing by himself;"*
> (John 5:19 NIV)

Before Jesus' crucifixion, Pilate asked Jesus, *"Don't you realize I have the power either to free you or to crucify you?"* Jesus' answer was simple, revealing, and full of Truth . . . *"You would have no power over me if it were not given to you from above"* (John 19:11 NIV).

Regardless of what storm we're facing in life, we can never forget the simple truth: *God is in charge.* As difficult as it is for us to understand, God's will in our lives has far greater purposes than we can imagine; yet, all of them are designed for greater good. We must face the Truth that says God is *ultimately* in control.

In understanding God's ways, we cannot decide to heartily accept some Truths, yet readily discount others. We must accept God's ways and trust in them; it's a decision we make that isn't based upon our desires or emotions. We walk by faith in our loving God. Take a moment to really grasp the following truth in Romans 9: 15-19 (NIV):

For he says to Moses, "I will have mercy on whom I have mercy, and I will have compassion on whom I have compassion." It does not, therefore, depend on man's desire or effort, but on God's mercy. For the Scripture says to Pharaoh: "I raised you up for this very purpose, that I might display my power in you and that my name might be proclaimed in all the earth." Therefore God has mercy on whom he wants to have mercy, and he hardens whom he wants to harden. One of you will say to me: "Then why does God still blame us? For who resists his will?" But who are you, O man, to talk back to God? "Shall what is formed say to him who formed it, 'Why did you make me like this?' "Does not the potter have the right to make out of the same lump of clay some pottery for noble purposes and some for common use?"

Even though our storms may come filled with pain and suffering, we are to clearly understand that they come from a loving God . . . and we must praise Him . . . *in* the storm.

> *God is not with you*
> *to keep the storms from coming . . .*
> *He's with you*
> *to take you through them.*

"Should we accept only good things from the hand of God and never anything bad?" (Job 2:10 NLT)

An unknown poet expressed the depths of God's work in and through us in this way:

When God wants to drill a man,
And thrill a man, And skill a man;
When God wants to mold a man
To play the noblest part,
Then he yearns with all his heart
To create so great and bold a man
That all the world shall be amazed,
Watch his methods, watch his ways —

How he ruthlessly perfects
Whom he royally elects.
How he hammers him and hurts him,
And with mighty blows, converts him
Into trial shapes of clay
Which only God understands.
While his tortured heart is crying,
And he lifts beseeching hands.
How he bends but never breaks
When his good he undertakes.
How he uses Whom he chooses,
And with every purpose, fuses him,
By every act, induces him
To try his splendor out.
God knows what he's about.

(We need to fully grasp what this poet did, God is at work, He has a purpose, and *He knows what He's doing*.)

One of God's primary purposes for our storms that we *can* understand is: He wants to transform us into the likeness of Christ.

> *For those God foreknew he also predestined*
> *to be conformed to the likeness of his Son, . . .*
> (Romans 8:29 NIV)

He is molding us, so that our character mirrors that of Jesus: the way He thinks, loves, and forgives. Through the process, He is teaching us to depend on His presence, instead of relying on our own strength. We are to draw *all* of our strength from Him (John 15:5):

"I am the vine; you are the branches.
If a man remains in me and I in him,
he will bear much fruit;
apart from me you can do nothing."

As God works on our character, He uses our suffering to teach us to keep focused upon Him. God's incredible love for us does not eliminate the pain, suffering, and heartache that we might go through; but, His Promises assure us that He is with us, and He is using it all for good (Romans 8:28). Through it all, we learn to trust that no matter how devastating the storm might be . . . God is with us. And if we trust and obey Him, He will strengthen us and fill us with hope in the *midst* of the storm.

"We do not know what to do, but our eyes are upon you."
(2 Chronicles 20:12 NIV)

You see, His presence is made perfect in your weakness; it is in your weakest moments where He will comfort you, strengthen you, and reassure you of His faithfulness. He wants you to know that He is not in your life to stop the storms from coming, but to take you through them . . . **He wants your faith.**

And it is impossible to please God without faith.
Anyone who wants to come to him must believe
that God exists and that he rewards
those who sincerely seek him.
(Hebrews 11:6 NLT)

God's Presence in the Storm

We can be certain that God would never test our faith and then push us out to sea without His presence. The question is, "Do *you* acknowledge His presence during these storms of life?" The even greater question is, *"At what point* do you acknowledge His presence?" We storm the gates of heaven, wondering, *"Where is God?"* Yet, we fail to see that He is there with us . . . *and He's been there all along.* In fact, He's in the clouds—He's hovering over us each day, going before us, preparing a way through the storm.

> *You can't allow your vision*
> *to become clouded with doubt and fear.*
> *Don't lose sight of the fact that God*
> *is with you always . . .*
> *He's been with you all along.*

The cloud of the Lord was over them
by day when they set out from the camp.
(Numbers 10:34 NIV)

They have heard that You, O Lord, are in the midst
of this people, for You, O Lord, are seen eye to eye, while
Your cloud stands over them; and You go before them in
a pillar of cloud by day and in a pillar of fire by night.
(Numbers 14:14 NASB)

Just think about the fact that the Disciples were in a boat, with who they supposedly believed was the Son of God; yet, even *they* failed to acknowledge Him, until it was almost too late. They were about to die! Why didn't it occur to them to ask for Jesus' help sooner? From the outside looking in, the answer seemed so obvious. In our own storms of life, it's often difficult to see the "obvious." Our vision becomes clouded with debilitating doubt and paralyzing fear.

The Disciples had seen Jesus perform many miracles—we have seen God work miracles in our own lives, yet we so easily forget them. Jesus says, *"Don't you remember"* (Matthew 16:9)? If they had faith in Him, the answer would be obvious—ask the Son of God to calm the storm! But they didn't. God knew that the Disciples' faith would grow through this experience. Their greater faith would enable them to be better witnesses. The miracles He performed were to teach us to have faith in Him, regardless of our circumstances—no matter how impossible things might seem.

God reminds us through His Word:

> *"Everything is possible for him who believes."*
> (Mark 9:23 NIV)

> *"Have faith in God."*
> (Mark 11:22 NIV)

The message God has for *you* is no different than it was for the Disciples. He wants you to know that faith in Him can bring about miracles in your life.

Many of us believe that miracles won't happen to us. Or maybe we're like the Disciples and we think that we have the ability to make it through this storm on our own. But, when we can't seem to rescue ourselves, we finally, as a last ditch effort, ask for God's help. Hear this truth: *"You don't have to save yourself."* (Besides, you can't!) Jesus came so that you don't have to . . . *He's the one who saves you through every storm of life.* He is all you need.

> *Hear this truth:*
> *"You don't have to save yourself."*
> *(Besides, you can't!)*
> *Jesus came so that you don't have to . . .*
> *He's the one who saves you through every*
> *storm of life. He is all you need.*

We tend to wait until the last moment because we seem to think that God can't possibly intervene in our situation. How much peace do we forfeit by struggling for the answers on our own? How much pain do we needlessly bear because we agonize over possibilities that never happen? We tend to believe that there are some things that God can handle, but we're convinced that on many things . . . *He needs our help.* At other times, we're certain that it's necessary for us to take control . . . God just seems to be taking too long. Even the Disciples, at some point, subconsciously believed that there was nothing that Jesus could do to help them calm the wind and waves of the storm. It was the perfect set up for the perfect miracle. *God knows what He's doing.*

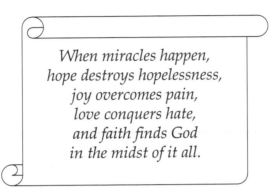

When miracles happen,
hope destroys hopelessness,
joy overcomes pain,
love conquers hate,
and faith finds God
in the midst of it all.

In the storm, He's bringing us to a place of embracing the truth that our life is better managed by His hands, not our own. Trust Him—He does a much better job than we could ever do.

In the face of impossible circumstances, God says, "Lift up your eyes. Look beyond the visible realities." God doesn't work in the "natural." He works in the "*super*natural." His only requirement is that we are no longer "unbelieving," but "believing." He says, "*Believe and have faith that I am at work*, and I will enrich your life beyond your imagination." Do you dare believe God? When miracles happen, hope destroys hopelessness, joy overcomes pain, love conquers hate, and *faith finds God in the midst of it all* . . . ever present . . . worthy of praise.

Who doesn't want a miracle? Who doesn't want to be saved from the paralyzing grip of fear? We beg God for a miracle, but when He shows up, we're often found with very little faith — we're like the Disciples, standing in awe and amazement. Our faith should never be surprised to see God's hand, when we've come to a place of surrender.

In our world, becoming mature means becoming

> *Our faith should never be surprised*
> *to see God when He shows up.*

"independent." In our spiritual journey, maturity means becoming *helplessly dependent upon God.* Our peace in the storm can only come from our resignation into God's hands. Regardless of how hopeless a situation might seem, we must surrender all of our hopes and expectations into His hands; when we do, we find that He will empower us to endure any hardship. His desire is that we would continue the journey without fear or anxiety, while trusting in His care. The more resigned we are to God's care, the less power our circumstances have over us. When we're resigned to God's care, we won't be frightened by undesirable news, and we won't be trying to constantly figure out the next step. If we have faith in God, we will simply trust, wait, and *expect* God.

Such people will not be overcome by evil. Those who are righteous will be long remembered. <u>They do not fear bad news; they confidently trust the LORD to care for them</u>. They are confident and fearless and can face their foes triumphantly. (Psalm 112:6-8 NLT)

Quite possibly, you're not sure that you want to take that step. You might feel that "trusting God" comes with too much obligation. You might decide that you don't want to feel a burden of having to "repay" God for His miracle in your life. You may desire His hand, but you're not sure about coming face to face with Him (Job 23:15). You may be overwhelmed in feeling that you would be in debt to Him and you don't want to carry that weight. The truth is that you're already in deeper debt to Him than you'll ever imagine; that's why He sent Jesus. *Jesus can save you.* It's the storms of your life that bring you to a place of surrender. God wants you to stop all of your "trying" and simply start "trusting." He wants to eliminate the fleshly part of you that wants to control your life. He wants you to encounter something much more wonderful than anything you could devise. When you truly understand your storms of life, you will find that your storms will allow God to lift you up and give you true life to the full . . . *until it overflows.*

It's possible that if we never had to face our storms of life we wouldn't seek the Lord. The purpose of your storm, simply put, is all about your relationship with Jesus. It's all out your faith in Him.

> *The more resigned we are to God's care, the less power our circumstances have over us.*

In John Ortberg's book, *Faith and Doubt*, he defines our faith and hope by saying that, *"Hope points to one Man, one hope, one God who is worth trusting, not because of who He is. He is the one in whom and by whom we can hope."* Faith looks Jesus in the eyes and says, *"Yes Lord, wherever You lead . . . I will follow."* We can trust that if He leads us into a raging storm, or allows a storm to come into our lives, He's got something amazing in mind. He wants to show you His sufficiency, His comforting presence, and His strength that will help you endure. Your *trials* become *tools* in the hand of God. Tell Him you'll follow Him — *then watch Him go to work.*

Then Jesus said to the Disciples,
"If any of you wants to be my follower,
you must put aside your selfish ambition,
shoulder your cross and follow me.
If you try to keep your life for yourself, you will lose it.
But if you give up your life for me, you will find true life."
(Mark 8:34-35 NLT)

When you bow down before the Lord and admit your dependence on him, he will lift you up and give you honor. (James 4:10 NLT)

The Call of the Storm

Storms of life are used by God to strengthen your faith in Him. He's asking you to step out in faith and show Him that you are ready to live with Him forever.

The storms call us to a higher place—they prove our faith and mature us spiritually. God may or may not have sent the storm into our life, but we can rest assured that He is with us through it all.

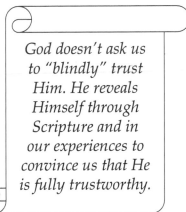

God doesn't ask us to "blindly" trust Him. He reveals Himself through Scripture and in our experiences to convince us that He is fully trustworthy.

The more we trust Him, the more our faith will grow. Placing our trust in Him will make all the difference for the journey.

Don't make the mistake of basing your faith on a particular outcome. We've all done it. We've prayed for God to answer our prayers with very detailed expectations, and we've seen our faith crumble to pieces when things didn't happen the way we thought they should. We find ourselves embracing "positive thinking," instead of real faith. Faith that grows us trusts in "Someone" rather than "something." Faith trusts in the character of God who is merciful, loving, and just. God doesn't ask us to "blindly" trust Him. He reveals Himself through Scripture and through our experiences to convince us that He *is* trustworthy.

> *Your storms of life will*
> ***reveal,***
> ***refine,***
> ***strengthen,***
> *and* ***perfect***
> *those areas that are hindering*
> *your spiritual growth.*

The call of the storms in your life is to have greater faith in God. Your circumstances might look hopeless, you may have cried out to God for help, and you may have only heard a deafening silence; but, in your moments of abandoning all hope, you will find yourself in awe and amazement when you witness the power of God in your life. Your momentary pain and suffering will vanish, in an instant, when you open your soul to the risks of faith. Faith in God will bring you to the edge . . . *every time*. Each step of faith will demand that you reach out for the hand of God. He wants you to be a witness to His awesome presence and power.

The call of the storm in the Disciples' lives caused them to be devoted witnesses to Christ because they experienced a "personal" miracle through the magnificent power of God—Jesus calmed their storm . . . He saved their lives.

*Then Jesus told him, "You believe because you have seen me. Blessed are those who **haven't seen me** and **believe anyway**." (John 20:29 NLT)*

> *Faith in God will bring you to the edge . . .*
> *every time. Each step of faith you take will demand*
> *that you reach out for the hand of God . . .*
> *make sure you take it and never let go.*

When trying to understand how this miracle relates to your life and the storms you face, it is important to realize that the storm did not slowly subside or die down—when the Disciples cried out to Jesus for help . . . it stopped immediately! It appears that from that moment on, the Disciples were overwhelmed, not only with the power that Jesus possessed, but that He truly must be the Son of God. When the Disciples witnessed this great miracle, they were suddenly overcome by its "stillness." Imagine being more frightened of how your storm of life is "stilled," rather than of the fear of the raging storm itself!

Can you imagine? Whatever storm you're currently in, God can stop it *immediately*. When we call
upon the name of Jesus, He does hear us; He will answer us through the storm. Will you call upon Him
now? Will you show Him your faith in Him and cry
out to Him even when you cannot see Him? *Or will
you keep trying to bail water out of a boat that is already
capsizing?*

> *Behind every storm there is a blessing.*
> *View your storm as a revelation from God,*
> *an opportunity to learn to trust Him,*
> *and a stepping stone for better*
> *things in the future.*

The Disciples were truly the closest men to the
Son of God; yet, at the end of this miracle we see that
even they had doubts in their heart about who Jesus
really was. They saw with their own eyes all of the
miracles He performed, but they still asked, *"Who is
this man?"* A little surprising . . . don't you think? On-
lookers may have believed that the Disciples must
have had the highest level of faith—they left their
lives and followed Jesus. But, Jesus knew where their
faith was lacking. Jesus saw their hearts . . . just like
He sees yours. You cannot hide your heart from God.

"The Lord looks at the heart."
(1 Samuel 16:7 NLT)

(typeof

It is in our storms where the areas of our lives that are hindering our spiritual growth are revealed. It is in the storms that God will reveal, refine, strengthen, and perfect those areas . . . if you allow Him to take you through the storm.

You can trust God. He already knows exactly what He's going to do in your situation. He has a plan. He wants you to place your trust in Him by saying, *"You are God, and nothing is impossible with You. I am giving this situation to You and it is no longer mine but yours to deal with as You will."* He's taking your faith to a place of understanding His desire and ability to work a miracle for you—not only in your current storm, but in every storm you will ever face. His desire is that you would develop an unwavering faith that is *anchored* in Him.

Trust in, lean on, rely on, and have confidence in Him at all times, you people; pour out your hearts before Him. God is a refuge for us (a fortress and a high tower). Selah [pause, and calmly think of that]!
(Psalm 62:8 AMP)

The Blessing Behind the Storm

It should be comforting to know that although God allows the storm, Jesus is in the boat with you. Yes, He is with you, right now, in the boat where you sit in the midst of your storm. The difference is: He is in

the stern resting because He knows the blessing behind all of the wind and rain. He knows that the destruction in your life can be used to rebuild your life
and make it better than it was before. He knows that
God has the power to turn your ashes to beauty.

*To all who mourn in Israel, he will give beauty for ashes,
joy instead of mourning, praise instead of despair. For the
Lord has planted them strong and graceful oaks for his
own glory.* (Isaiah 61:3 NLT)

There is no storm that is not permitted and con-
trolled by God. When Jesus rose from the dead, He
overcame every spirit in opposition to Him. By His
resurrection, Jesus proclaimed power over all de-
monic forces in your life. This means that whatever
your storm is, God has allowed it, and it has been
overcome through Christ—just knowing this should
bring about a great blessing in your spirit. Behind
every storm there is a blessing—God has assured us
there is one. Why not view this time as a revelation
from God, an opportunity to learn to trust Him, and
a stepping stone to better things in the future. He's
assured us:

*God blesses the people
who patiently endure testing.*
(James 1:12 NLT)

For the Disciples, their blessing was acquiring greater faith in God which made them the greatest witnesses for Christ—what a blessing for you and I! When God allows a storm in your life . . . it has great purpose; if you miss the purpose, you may miss God's will for your life.

> *Your storms are more than just the pain and suffering on the surface. Your storms are tools in the hand of God — He's working to bring about miracles in your life.*

Every intimate part of our lives is no surprise to God. Many times, when He leads us into the storms, He's leading us to a place of surrender and complete dependence upon Him. The storms aren't necessarily to show us His incredible powers; although His love, mercy, and grace continually amaze even those with incredible faith. God doesn't have to prove His power, just as He doesn't have to prove His existence—it's the obvious. We just have to open our eyes and look around us. We don't have to go very far to realize there is an amazing God who keeps the world in motion, and He has addressed every intricate detail which sustains life here on earth.

God is more interested in showing us the heart of who He is. God wants us to understand that our storms are more than just storms. They are more than just the pain and suffering on the surface. Our storms build a bridge to an intimate relationship with Him. The storms just give God another opportunity to demonstrate His unconditional love for us.

He wants you to understand, firsthand, what it feels like to reach out and have His hand grasp yours. He wants you to understand what it's like to see His face and hear His voice. No one and nothing can simply give you this intimate understanding through witnessing.

> *You can rest assured through God's Promises that He will use every storm for your good and His greater purposes. God always has a plan. Trust Him — get to the back of the boat with Jesus.*

Others' relationship with God can you *lead* you to Him, but He does the rest. God wants a very personal relationship with you . . . He wants you to experience a miracle *in your own life.*

The Disciples had witnessed many miracles that Jesus had performed, yet they had not experienced a miracle for themselves; when Jesus calmed the storm, they were given a "personal" miracle.

God wants to give you greater knowledge of Himself, so that when the storms rage around you,

you can have peace because you have learned that He is in control and there is nothing to fear. He wants you to be assured that He is with you, He will carry you, and He is your refuge and source of strength.

God is our refuge and strength,
always ready to help in times of trouble.
(Psalm 46:1 NLT)

When you understand your storms and grasp the fact that Jesus is in your boat, you, too, can experience a miracle in your storm. When you seek out God's call to you through the storm, allowing Him to use it all for His purposes, your storms will bring about great blessings in your life. You'll even find that your storms of life will be used by God to bless the lives of others! You can rest assured through God's Promises...He will use *every* storm for your good and His greater purposes. God always has a plan. Trust Him. It's your life He wants to use, but He can't use you unless you're in the *back* of the boat with Jesus—at rest, trusting Him. So, the begging question is,

"Where are you in the boat right now?"

Scriptures to Encourage You in the Storm

These trials are only to test your faith, to show that it is strong and pure. It is being tested as fire tests and purifies gold — and your faith is far more precious to God than mere gold. So if your faith remains strong after being tried by fiery trials, it will bring you much praise and glory and honor on the day when Jesus Christ is revealed to the whole world. (1 Peter 1:7 NLT)

Draw close to God, and God will draw close to you. (James 4:8 NLT)

So, be truly glad! There is wonderful joy ahead, even though it is necessary for you to endure many trials for a while. (1 Peter 1:6 NLT)

I know the Lord is always with me. I will not be shaken, for he is right beside me. (Psalm 16:8 NLT)

So be strong and take courage, all you who put your hope in the Lord! (Psalm 31:24 NLT)

"For I know the plans I have for you," says the Lord. "They are plans for good and not for disaster, to give you a future and a hope. In those days when you pray, I will listen. If you look for me in earnest, you will find me when you seek me." (Jeremiah 29:11 NLT)

In quietness and in trusting confidence I find strength. (Isaiah 30:15 NLT)

We can rejoice, too, when we run into problems and trials, for we know that they are good for us – they help us learn strength of character in us, and character strengthens our confident expectations of salvation. And this expectation will not disappoint us for we know how dearly God loves us, because he has given us the Holy Spirit to fill our hearts with his love. (Romans 5:3 NLT)

So let us come boldly to the throne of our gracious God. There we will receive his mercy, and we will find grace to help us when we need it. (Hebrews 4:16 NLT)

God is our refuge and strength, always ready to help in times of trouble. (Psalm 46:1 NLT)

I have refined you but not in the way silver is refined. Rather, I have refined you in the furnace of suffering. I will rescue you for my sake, – yes, for my own sake! (Isaiah 48:10 NLT)

We are pressed on every side by troubles, but we are not crushed and broken. We are perplexed, but we don't give up and quit. We are hunted down, but God never abandons us. We get knocked down, but we get up again and keep going . . . (2 Corinthians 4: 8-10 NLT)

For you will rescue me from my troubles and help me to triumph . . . (Psalm 54:7 NLT)

We do not know what to do, but our eyes are upon you. (2 Chronicles 20:12 NLT)

So humble yourselves under the mighty power of God, and in his good time he will honor you. Give all your worries and cares to God, for he cares about what happens to you. (1 Peter 5:6-7 NLT)

Do not fear anything except the Lord Almighty. He alone is the Holy one. If you fear him, you need fear nothing else. He will keep you safe. (Isaiah 8: 12-14 NLT)

It was by faith that Moses left the land of Egypt, not fearing the king's anger. He kept right on going because he kept his eyes on the one who is invisible. (Hebrews 11:27-28 NLT)

In quietness and confidence is your strength. (Isaiah 30:15 NLT)

Chapter 2

⚓ Where are *You* in the Boat? ⚓

Storms of Life

In order to survive your storms of life, you must first identify where you are in the boat. Jesus was resting in the *back* of the boat in this storm. My guess is that, if you're like the rest of us, you're frantic and overwhelmed with fear and doubt when a storm of life is raging. In jest, if you were to look at your boat on the map of life, many times you would find your marker that says, "*You are Here . . .*" falling overboard.

Unfortunately, we often feel as though life is just one storm after another . . . for many, *this is reality*. As we anticipate the next storm that is sure to come along, we wonder what kind of destruction it will create and if there will be anything left in the aftermath. When our storm is raging, fear sets in and we get busy trying to keep our boat from capsizing. We start bailing water left and right—we exhaust ourselves to the point that we start looking for others to help us, instead of looking to *the only One who can.*

Like the Disciples, when decide to finally look to Jesus . . . we find Him resting! *How can He rest at a time like this?*

In the Back of the Boat

In our storms of life, the place God wants us to be is in the back of the boat with Jesus — *resting*. Our first reaction when we're overcome with fear is to take control. We want to do "something" and find a solution that will alleviate the pain and suffering that is draining our soul.

> *When our storm is raging, we get busy*
> *trying to keep our boat from capsizing;*
> *we start bailing water left and right,*
> *looking to anyone and everyone to help us.*
> *We fail to look to the only One who can.*

We're not much different from the Disciples on the boat, who were at the feet of Jesus every day, so we shouldn't judge our faith so harshly. A fallen world is a breeding ground for doubt.

At times, we even find enough nerve to start instructing God what to do about our situation! We don't hesitate to angrily cry out, "Do something! And by the way, do it *now*!" Somehow, we forget that God is in control. How easily that truth slips our minds in times of desperation.

God's throne isn't designed for "two." Trying to take over God's job is incredibly dangerous, at best. God doesn't need our help—He's more than qualified for the job. He's quite capable of handling whatever storm emerges in our lives. He wants us *in the back of the boat.*

The Disciples were fighting for their lives in their own abilities, instead of relying on the power of God. Amazingly, they needed to rely on the power that was lying right beside them! Jesus was with them through it all. From the moment the winds picked up . . . to the moment the waves threatened to drown them . . . *He was there all along.* He is with you, too. He has never left your side. *He never will.*

God's desire is for us to learn from this miracle and realize that His throne of grace is the first place we should go when a storm develops! Don't you think that after the storm was calmed, the Disciples were thinking, *"Wow, why didn't we just cry out to Jesus earlier?"* It sure would have saved them from experiencing such needless distress.

Satan loves to see us trying to take control by reaching out to anything and everything *except* Jesus. Satan knows that if he's given an opening . . . he can use it to separate us from God and destroy our lives. Storms in life seldom knock—*neither does Satan.* He won't send an announcement of his arrival, and you won't hear the door bell ring . . . *he feels more than comfortable letting himself in.* And he knows, all too well, that trying to control our lives is completely against God's will . . . *it leaves an open door.* How can we be in God's will, if we're living out our own will? A storm comes along and we become frantic. Instead of kneeling and praising our Creator, we scream up to the heavens, *"Why?"*

It's at this precise moment that we should be asking *"What?"* We should be asking, *"What do you want me to learn from this, Lord? How are you using this to bring me closer to You?"* Instead, we question, we doubt, and we beg for a way out. Don't try to maneuver your way out of whatever trial you're going through. God has purpose in it,

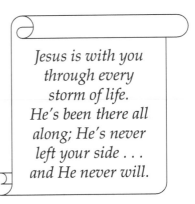

Jesus is with you through every storm of life. He's been there all along; He's never left your side . . . and He never will.

and He allows trials in the lives of those He dearly loves. ANYTHING that drives you to the foot of His Cross is worth EVERYTHING you'll have to go through in life. You see, He wants to give you something far greater than anything you can fathom . . . *persevering faith.*

It is through storms of life that the lost are saved, the addict suddenly becomes sober, and the sick are swiftly healed. Our darkest *hour* can become God's *moment* of power. It is through our faith alone that we are able to face afflictions and have confident hope. "Living by faith" means seeing God's hand in *all* of our troubles.

The faith that God wants you to have is not faith that *"believes until . . ."* It's the faith that doesn't quit, even if the answer does not come quickly, even if things get worse instead of better, and even if an answer *appears* impossible. When we're at wit's end, faith believes that God has already prepared a great work of deliverance and restoration. His greatest miracles in our lives will come when we're empty of solutions, when all our human efforts are in vain, and *only a miracle will calm our storm.*

> *ANYTHING that drives you to the foot of His Cross is worth EVERYTHING you'll have to go through in life. God wants to give you something far greater than your present pleasure . . . He's giving you the gift of persevering faith.*

Our faith is continually tested and tried (Job 7:18, Jeremiah 17:10, James 1:12). As the storms of our lives rage and God takes away all of our internal supports, we can be tempted to give up on the journey. We may even ask God to end it all in the most ultimate way.

"Why are you treating, your servant, so harshly?
Have mercy on me!" . . .
"If this is how you intend to treat me,
just go ahead and kill me.
Do me a favor and spare me this misery!"
(Numbers 11:11, 15 NLT)

We can find ourselves "dead in the water" before we even take *one* step of faith. We can become so easily overwhelmed that we throw in the towel before we even begin bailing water out of the boat. In our moment of despair, God's voice pierces through the clouds to say,

> *Persevering faith*
> *continues to believe God,*
> *even if the answer does not come quickly,*
> *even if things get worse instead of better,*
> *and even if an answer seems impossible.*

"Has my arm lost its power?
Now you will see whether or not
my word comes true!"
(Numbers 11:23 NLT)

Charles Spurgeon once said, *"The wilderness is the way to Canaan. Defeat prepares us for victory. The darkest hour of the night precedes the dawn."* Our most difficult time in faith is said to be the last half hour. Unless we're trusting God, unless we have persevering faith, unless we stop trying to understand and reason what His overall plan is, we will find ourselves in complete darkness. But if we develop the faith that perseveres, God promises that He will turn all of our darkness to light.

Light arises in the darkness for the upright, gracious, compassionate, and just [who are in right standing with God]. (Psalm 112:4 AMP)

God wants to develop persevering faith within you—He has purposes in every storm of your life. If God didn't see purpose in the storm you're in, He wouldn't allow you to be in the midst of it; to try to escape it would rob you of God's greatest work in your life. We must recognize that we are in the hands of a loving Father who has allowed all of the circumstances that have brought us to the storm front which will enable Him to teach us many needed truths.

You see, He wants to take you *through* it—not over it, not under it, not around it, not between it . . . *through it*. It is through the storm that we come to know God better. He is revealing Himself in greater ways—He's working *in and through* us, so that we can reflect His glory even more.

And all of us have had that veil removed so that we can be mirrors that brightly reflect the glory of the Lord. And as the Spirit of the Lord works within us, we become more and more like him and reflect his glory even more.
(2 Corinthians 3:18 NLT)

And we know that God causes everything to work together for the good of those who love God and are called according to his purpose for them. (Romans 8:28 NLT)

You see, it may not be what *we* want to go through and it may not happen in the timing *we* want to see it all done; but, God knows what's best and He'll use it all for His good! We must *believe Him*...His good is ultimately our good. *We just have to trust Him.*

It may be impossible to accept in times of unthinkable distress, but *God knows what He's doing*. He knows us better than we know ourselves. He knows about our future just as much as He's recorded our past. He knows every intricate detail of our lives from beginning to end. He knows the story of your life before it even begins. His knowledge is infinite. So, He knows how best to work our lives and our circumstances in harmony with His will. He knows exactly which storms will drive us to Him. We may not be able to grasp the slightest understanding of *"why"* we're going through what we're going through, *but we can trust God anyway.*

"My thoughts are completely different form yours,"
says the Lord. "And my ways are far beyond anything
you could imagine. For just as the heavens are higher
than the earth, so are my ways higher than your ways
and my thoughts higher than your thoughts."
(Isaiah 55:8-9 NLT)

Yet, even as we desperately try to step out in faith, our flesh still insists on asking the question, *"Why?"* Our soul begs the question, *"If God is God and He loves us, why would He allow this pain, this misery, this terror, this deep heartache, and these endless tears?"* Our memory fails us: God did not promise us a perfect life. In fact, He promised just the opposite:

"I have told you all this so that you may have peace in me.
Here on earth you will have many trials and sorrows.
But take heart, because I have overcome the world."
(John 16:33 NLT)

We're reminded, once again, that storms *will* come. But, what we need to know is that whatever our storm is . . . *God is there*. He knows our tears and sorrows, and He records each one of them in His book. God's heart is a heart that overflows with love. His heart not only breaks for you . . . *His heart breaks with you*. God cries tears for you, and He holds your tears in the palms of His hands.

You keep track of all my sorrows. You have collected all my tears in your bottle. You have recorded each one in your book. (Psalm 56:8 NLT)

The shortest, and arguably the most powerful, Scripture in the Bible expresses God's compassion:

Jesus wept.
(John 11:35 NIV)

His tears could flood the earth; *His love will flood your heart.* There isn't one moment of your life that He is not present in. He is in all places, at all times, and so is His consuming mercy and grace. He wants to comfort you and give you peace through the storm.

All praise to God, the Father of our Lord Jesus Christ. God is our merciful Father and the source of all comfort.
(2 Corinthians 1:3 NLT)

Bailing Water from the Boat

It's not surprising that so many of us feel like we're always bailing water—wearing ourselves out physically and emotionally. The bailing alone might even very well kill us. It seems that no matter how hard we work . . . *we're still going under.* At times, we even find ourselves putting water *in* the boat . . . when we really meant to take it out! We desperately reach out to others, believing that if we just had a little help . . . we'd have a chance of surviving.

Just like the Disciples in the boat, we believe we've made it through storms before and *we didn't have to call on God*. But, the truth is that God has rescued us many times and we just don't acknowledge it. We tend to believe that we just got "lucky" or that our survival through previous storms resulted from a series of "coincidences." It's been said that "coincidences" are God's way of remaining "anonymous." God is faithful. He is with us. Even when we let go, *He never does*.

How many times have you tried everything you know to make your storm go away, or at least subside a little, *without success*? The truth is that you'll never make it through alone. So ask yourself, *"Where am I in the boat?"* Are you constantly bailing water? Are you trying to call for help, but no one seems to hear you? Are you pretending to be resting, but so anxious inside that you feel like you're drowning?

Here's a revelation:
If you're constantly bailing water from your boat,
you're not trusting God and
you're not walking in His will.

The Lifeboat

If you're in the midst of a storm and you're bailing water at this very moment, *it's actually good news.* When we decide to stop bailing altogether . . . *that's when we're really in trouble!* We can come to a place of "giving up." We feel numb: We have difficulty eating and sleeping, we're unable to focus, we feel power-less and unworthy, and we're overwhelmed by eve-rything. Those feelings are indicators that you're go-ing under. So, when you're bailing, it shows that you still have hope within you . . . it's just that you're put-ting your hope in yourself, instead of God. When you're facing hopelessness, you need to reach out for the hand of God more than ever before.

> *Hope deferred makes the heart sick.*
> (Proverbs 13:12 NLT)

When we begin to lose hope, our lives take a det-rimental turn for the worse; we seek anything and everything to find temporary relief. And that's exact-ly what they are . . . *temporary.* We begin to find short term perceived solutions in alcohol, drugs, destruc-tive and meaningless relationships, and endless in-dulgences of the flesh. The sense of despair can seem so overwhelming that as the twenty foot waves come crashing in . . . we don't even have the strength to breathe. Yet, what we don't realize is that it's through those vices, we're only putting more water in a boat that is already sinking.

Losing hope is such a self–destructive response to life's problems. The only thing it does is reinforce everything that's wrong in life.

Your eye is a lamp for your body. A pure eye lets sunshine in your soul. But an evil eye shuts out the light and plunges you into the darkness. If the light you think you have is really darkness, how deep that darkness will be! (Matthew 6:22-23 NLT)

He floods darkness with light;
he brings light to the deepest gloom. (Job 12:22 NLT)

My comfort in my suffering is this:
Your promise preserves my life. (Psalm 119:50 NIV)

So why do we lose hope? There are many reasons, but mostly we lose hope because our own expectations for our lives are not fulfilled. *We decide* what will make us happy . . . what will make us complete; when

> *These trying times are God's way to ultimately allow us to reach the end of our will and begin to accept His.*

those dreams don't become reality, we feel an incredible sense of loss that can become debilitating. When we feel unfulfilled in some way . . . it seems much better to give up hope, than to continue experiencing the pain of our losses. All hope can be destroyed in an instant, when we realize that our joy is secured in a relationship, the success of our career, whether or not we can have children, if our spouse makes us happy, whether or not our children come home for the holidays, what kind of home we live in, what kind of clothes we wear, or what kind of car we drive. When the reality of our *lack of control* in our lives finally hits . . . *despair and loss of hope is the result.*

If you're in your boat right now bailing water and you're thinking of throwing in the bucket, fully understand these Scriptures,

No discipline is enjoyable while it is happening —
it is painful! But afterward there will be a quiet harvest
of right living for those who are trained in this way.
(Hebrews 12:11 NLT)

Even if I caused you sorrow by my letter, I do not regret it.
Though I did regret it — I see that my letter hurt you,
but only for a little while — yet now I am happy,
not because you were made sorry, but because your sorrow
led you to repentance. For you became sorrowful as God
intended and so were not harmed in any way by us.
Godly sorrow brings repentance that leads to salvation
and leaves no regret, but worldly sorrow brings death.
(2 Corinthians 7:8-10 NIV)

These times of struggling and bailing water from our capsizing boats are times to come to the end of ourselves and be reminded that we are to rely on God alone. These "trying" times are God's way to ultimately allow us to reach the end of our will and begin to accept His. Paul reminds us in 2 Corinthians 12:7-10 (NLT):

But to keep me from getting puffed up, I was given a thorn in my flesh a messenger from Satan to torment me and keep me from getting proud. Three different times I begged the Lord to take it away. Each time he said, "My gracious favor is all you need. My power works best in your weakness." So now I am glad to boast about my weaknesses, so that the power of Christ may work through me. Since I know it is all for Christ's good, I am quite content with my weaknesses and with insults, hardships, persecutions, and calamities. For when I am weak, then I am strong.

Paul helps us to realize that these storms that we are going through are *exactly* where God needs us, in order to bring about our good and fulfill His greater purposes.

While we're in the midst of our storm, it is the opportunity for God to ask us to evaluate what's "on board" and determine what can be tossed over! In the Scriptures, it speaks of a time where Paul experienced a raging storm. He shows us what it means to always trust in God . . . *even if we end up shipwrecked for a period of time.*

The next day, as gale–force winds continued to batter the ship, the crew began throwing cargo overboard. The following day they even threw out the ship's equipment and anything else they could lay their hands on. The terrible storm raged unabated for many days, blotting out the sun and stars, until at last all hope was gone. No one had eaten for a long time. Finally, Paul called the crew together and said, "Men, you should have listened to me in the first place and not left Fair Havens. You would have avoided all this injury and loss. But take courage! None of you will lose your lives, even though the ship will go down. For last night an angel of the God to whom I belong and whom I serve stood beside me, and he said, 'Do not be afraid, Paul, for you will surely stand trial before Caesar! What's more, God in his goodness has granted safety to everyone sailing with you.' So take courage! For I believe God. It will be just as he said. But we will be shipwrecked on an island. (Acts 27:18-26 NLT)

So, what extra "cargo" do you have on board your boat? Maybe, like many who have emailed me through ScriptureNow.com, it's a destructive relationship, deepening debt, sinful habits, or just a negative attitude. Whatever it is . . . if you keep hanging on to it in your boat, you're going to sink. Being shipwrecked is much better than going under! At least if you're shipwrecked, you're still able to be rescued!

In this particular account of Paul's journey, we're shown a clear example of how Satan creates doubt when we're desperate and relying on God's promises to carry us through the storms of life. You see, even after Paul had assured his crew that God promised they would live, the crew sensed they were headed for the rocks — in an attempt to escape, they let the lifeboat down into the sea.

About midnight on the fourteenth night of the storm, as we were being driven across the sea of Adria, the sailors sensed land was near. They took soundings and found that the water was only 120 feet deep. A little later they sounded again and found only 90 feet. At this rate they were afraid that they would soon be driven against the rocks along the shore, so they threw out four anchors from the back of the ship. But Paul said to the commanding officers and the soldiers, "You will die unless the sailors stay aboard." So the soldiers cut the ropes and let the boat fall off. (They let the "lifeboats" go and as the story continues, everyone escaped safely to shore) (Acts 27:27-32 NLT parenthetical comments mine.)

So often, we are just like the crew of this ship. When a storm hits, we see danger ahead and believe there is no way we'll make it through . . . *even when God promises that we will.* We suddenly panic and reach out for some kind of lifeboat, instead of God who is the only One who can truly rescue us.

One thing we need to know in our walk of faith, as we grasp the truth that "the darkest hour comes just before the dawn," is that it's at "midnight" when desperation is at its peak. It's in the last moments of the day, when we feel as though the storm is about to take us under, we are to stand in faith and praise God.

> *At midnight I rise to praise you . . .*
> (Psalm 119:62 ESV)

> *Around midnight Paul and Silas*
> *were praying and singing hymns to God,*
> *and the other prisoners were listening.*
> (Acts 16:25 NLT)

It's at "midnight," when all hope seems gone, we are to call upon God and praise Him. Your testimony in the storms of your life is giving glory to God, as others watch the crashing waves threaten to swallow you. It was at midnight that Paul and Silas began praising God from behind the prison walls; it was then . . . *God showed up.* He often shows up in the midnight hour . . . when nothing else, but His awesome, mighty power is able to rescue us.

Suddenly there was a great earthquake, so that the very foundations of the prison were shaken; and at once all the doors were opened and everyone's shackles were unfastened. (Acts 16:26 AMP)

Did you catch that? *Suddenly*. There's that word again. "*Suddenly*" God moves — He is all we need. So, it's time to let go of those lifeboats in our lives — we don't need them. We need to let go of those things that are a "temporary rescue:" alcohol, drugs, self indulgence, and pride. God's Promises through His Word are all that can truly rescue us and bring us into a life of peace and salvation — *if* we stay in the boat! Besides, you don't need a "lifeboat" when you have Jesus — He's your "lifeguard." He's the *ultimate* lifeguard because He "walks on water!"

> *"You never know Jesus is all you need,*
> *until Jesus is all you've got."*
> *God is taking everything, so that you'll*
> *be left with all that He offers . . .*
> *abundant peace and joy through His grace.*

But, Jesus is not only our "Lifeguard," He is also called our "Anchor." It is our hope in Jesus Christ, the Living Word, who is the *"anchor of our souls."*

[Now] we have this [hope] as a sure and steadfast anchor of the soul [it cannot slip and it cannot break down under whoever steps out upon it — a hope] that reaches farther and enters [the very certainty of the Presence] within the veil. (Hebrews 6:19 AMP)

The times in our lives when we feel overwhelmed, as if we are going to drown, are the times when we get desperate with God. It's in these times of being "prisoners" of hopelessness that we should renew our minds through God's Word . . . and become *prisoners of hope.* God promises that He will restore double what we have lost, when we trust in Him.

Return to the stronghold [of security and prosperity],
you prisoners of hope; even today do I declare that
I will restore double your former prosperity to you.
(Zechariah 9:12 AMP)

Unfortunately, it usually takes a raging storm to reveal what is really important in life and get us back in line with what God's will is for our lives. In the words of a wise old saint, *"You never know Jesus is all you need, until Jesus is all you've got."* So when you wonder why you're bailing water all the time, realize this: God is taking everything you've got, so that you'll be left with all that He offers . . . abundant peace and joy through His grace.

Let us not forget, whatever our storm is, whatever our circumstances might be, there is no situation that is too difficult for God. We don't need a "lifeboat" — we have a Savior that walks on water!

I cried out, "I'm slipping!" and your unfailing love,
O Lord supported me. When doubts filled my mind,
your comfort gave me hope and cheer.
(Psalm 94:19 NLT)

Scriptures to Encourage You in the Storm

I cried out to the Lord in my suffering, and he heard me. He set me free from all my fears. For the Angel of the Lord guards all who fear him, and he rescues them.
(Psalm 34:6-7 NLT)

God guards me, keeps me in perfect and constant peace because my mind is stayed on Him, because I commit myself to Him, lean on Him, and hope confidently in Him.
(Isaiah 26:3 NLT)

The Lord says, "I will rescue those who love me. I will protect those who trust in my name. When they call on me, I will answer; I will be with them in trouble. I will rescue them and honor them. I will satisfy them with a long life and give them salvation." (Psalm 91:14-16 NLT)

This is why we never give up. Though our bodies are dying, our spirits are being renewed every day. For our present troubles are quite small and won't last very long. Yet they produce for us an immeasurably great glory that will last forever! So we don't look at the troubles we can see right now; rather, we look forward to what we have not yet seen. For the troubles we see will soon be over, but the joys to come will last forever. (2 Corinthians 4:16-17 NLT)

I know the Lord is always with me.
I will not be shaken, for he is right beside me.
(Psalm 16:8 NLT)

So don't worry about tomorrow, for tomorrow will bring its own worries. Today's trouble is enough for today. (Matthew 6:34 NLT)

In his kindness God called you to his eternal Glory by means of Jesus Christ. After you have suffered a little while, he will restore, support, and strengthen you, and he will place you on a firm foundation. All power is his forever and ever. Amen. (1 Peter 5:10-11 NLT)

For if you carefully obey the law and regulations that the Lord gave to Israel through Moses, you will be successful. Be strong and courageous; do not be afraid or lose heart! (1 Chronicles 22:13 NLT)

Now glory be to God! By his mighty power at work within us, he is able to accomplish infinitely more than we would ever dare to ask or hope. (Ephesians 3:20 NLT)

For the eyes of the Lord run to and fro throughout the whole earth, to show Himself strong on behalf of those whose heart is loyal to Him. (2 Chronicles 16:9 NLT)

Show me the path where I should walk, O Lord; point out the right road for me to follow. Lead me by your truth and teach me, for you are the God who saves me. All day long I put my hope in you. (Psalm 25:4-5 NLT)

God blesses the people who patiently endure testing. (James 1:12)

No, dear brothers and sisters, I am still not all I should be, but I am focusing all my energies on this one thing: Forgetting the past and looking forward to what lies ahead, I strain to reach the end of the race and receive the prize for which God, through Christ Jesus, is calling us up to heaven. (Philippians 3:13-14 NLT)

My trust and assured reliance and confident hope is fixed in Him. (Hebrews 2:13 NLT)

So if you are suffering according to God's will, keep on doing what is right, and trust yourself to the God who made you, for he will never fail you. (1 Peter 4:19 NLT)

I will be happy when the way is rough, because it gives my patience a chance to grow. So I will let it grow, and not try to squirm out of my problems. For when my patience is finally in full bloom, then I will be ready for anything, strong in character, full and complete. (James 1: 2-4 NLT)

Chapter 3

⚓ Lord, Don't You Care? ⚓

A Silent Savior

When the Disciples had finally come to the end of themselves on the Sea of Galilee, they desperately and bitterly cried out to Jesus:

> *Jesus was in the stern, sleeping on a cushion.*
> *The disciples woke him and said to him,*
> *"Teacher, don't you care if we drown?"*
> (Mark 4:28 NIV)

How many times have you asked the question not only to God, but to others around you, *"Don't you care?"* So often, we feel all alone; as though no one cares. We share our struggles and sorrows with family, friends, and even complete strangers. We engage *anyone* who will listen. The question is, "Are we sharing it all with God?" — *the only One who truly cares.* And when we do cry out to Him . . . do we hear His answer?

More importantly than sharing our heart with God, He desires to share His heart with us and give us peace in knowing that He loves us and cares about every intricate detail of our lives.

> *Jesus wasn't just telling the storm, "Peace! Be Still!" . . . He was teaching us to "Be Still."*

Still . . . the begging question remains, *"Does God Care?"* We find the answer in the message of this miracle when Jesus calmed the storm. Jesus wasn't just telling the storm, "Peace! Be Still!" He was teaching *us* to "Be Still." So, when we ask if He cares, He says, "Yes, Be Still."

> *Be still,*
> *and know that I am God . . .*
> (Psalm 46:10 NLT)

According to Webster's Dictionary, to "be still" is "to devoid of or abstain from motion, uttering no sound, quiet, subdued, muted, calm, or tranquil." "Being still" can cause us to think of the "calm" that was brought about by this miracle. But, it seems that we are even better able to understand "being still" and "being calm" in describing what they *are not*: agitation, fear, or turbulence. We would never know "calm," unless there were a counterforce to cause us to notice it. Likewise, we'd never learn to "Be Still" if we never had a storm in our life.

In talking about such definitions, and our storms of life, it seems only fitting to mention the Beaufort Scale. If you're not familiar with it … it's a scale that was developed over many years (first developed in

> *God wants us to be "Calm," even though the storm may rage at "Hurricane Force." Where would the Beaufort Scale register the winds of your soul?*

1806), primarily for those traveling the seas.

It was incredibly difficult to gage weather conditions when the communication that was being used was so subjective; one's understanding of "a stiff breeze" might be another's "soft breeze." Therefore, the Scale was continually developed to the point of creating a formula that would enable universal understanding. On one end of the Scale's spectrum is "Calm," and on the other end is "Hurricane Force" (which is *past* "Violent Storm").

So, even in our storms of life, we could look at the Beaufort Scale and get an indication of what kind of storm we're in and how "calm" we are as the storm rages. Some of our storms may start very low on the Scale, while others may move immediately past the

"Violent Storm" level. Regardless, God wants *us* to be in the "Calm" area of the Scale, even though the storm may rage at "Hurricane Force." The question God has for you is, *"Where would the Beaufort Scale register the winds of your soul?"*

> *It is only when we're "still" that we can draw near to God, hear His voice, and be certain that He cares.*

Our problem is that usually when storms arise, we get moving . . . and fast! Our soul drives the Scale, taking a "Calm" reading to "Hurricane Force" in a matter of moments—even when the actual storm may only be registering "Strong Breeze." Our emotions run high and we become frantic to find a solution. We demand answers to the begging questions, *"Why is this happening? How will I get through this? When will I be rescued?"*

We continue to challenge God's will for our lives by repeatedly questioning His sovereignty; more than that, we question the genuineness of His love. We certainly don't question Him as much when He's pouring down blessings upon us! Why do we insist on giving into our flesh by demanding a way out of it all? If God wanted us out, *He'd make a way.* Do we ever really get anywhere by trying to force life to happen in the way we want it to?

God has *purposes* in the storms . . . one of which is to grow an intimate relationship with us. God knows that we struggle to put Him above all else in our lives. We place a higher priority on our connection with family and friends, rather than on our relationship with Him. We can even allow finances, work, and endless personal pleasures to interfere. When God sees us drifting away, He may use a storm to draw us back to Him . . . so that we will refocus.

> *There are some lessons that can only be learned in our storms of life . . . God knows what He's doing.*

God was teaching the Disciples, when life got turbulent, they were to keep their eyes on Jesus. Sometimes, there are lessons that can only be learned in the storms of life — *God knows what He's doing.*

It's only when we are "still" that we can draw near to God, hear His voice, and be certain that He cares. We can't even *begin* to hear His voice if our soul is registering "Violent Storm" on the Beaufort Scale. If this is where our faith is in our storms, the Scale tells us: the waves are covering us, the winds are over sixty-four miles per hour, and our visibility is severely reduced. Step out into a storm like that and find out if you're even able to see your hand in front of you . . . much less be able to keep your balance in order to remain standing. One thing is for sure, it would be incredibly difficult to take a step forward . . . especially when you can't see where you're going. If your soul (mind, will, and emotions) is going through a "Hurricane Force" storm, it is nearly impossible to take a step of faith.

We'll miss God's miracles for us when we're focused on the storm, instead of Him. If God wants to grow our intimacy with Him, we have to learn how we communicate with Him. We can go to Him through prayer — where He hears us. But, we must also find a way to hear *His voice*, when we can't see through the treacherous wind and rain.

In order to hear Him through the storm that rages, we must redirect our attention to His Word . . . **that's where He speaks.** God's voice is still and quiet.

> *"It stood still, but I could not discern its appearance;*
> *A form was before my eyes;*
> **There was silence, then I heard a voice:"**
> (Job 4:16 NASB)

And He said, Go out and stand on the mount before the Lord. And behold, the Lord passed by, and a great and strong wind rent the mountains and broke in pieces the rocks before the Lord, but the Lord was not in the wind; and after the wind an earthquake, but the Lord was not in

*the earthquake; and after the earthquake a fire, but the Lord was not in the fire; **and after the fire [a sound of gentle stillness and] a still, small voice.***
(1 Kings 19: 11-12 AMP)

> *In order to hear God's voice, we must fix our eyes on Jesus who perfects our faith.*

God's voice comes through His Word, and it comes as spontaneous thoughts, visions, feelings, or impressions. It comes after spending time in His presence . . . through constant prayer and meditation. If you're uncertain as to whether or not you're hearing from God, you can continue to search His Word, in order to confirm what He has spoken to you.

Unfortunately, in our "noisy" world, Christians have lost the ability to understand when they are hearing from God. We've lost sight of God's greatest desire . . . that we would *"know Him."*

*Now this is eternal life:
that they may know you,
the only true God, and Jesus Christ,
whom you have sent.*
(John 17:3 NIV)

Though we have the promise, "*My sheep hear My voice* (John 10:27)," so many believers are starved for the intimate relationship with God which can satisfy the longing desires of their hearts. In the storms of our lives, we desperately need to hear God's voice. It's imperative that we build our relationship with God, in such a way, so that we will be inclined to hear Him when the waves are crashing in on us and our faith is being shaken to its core.

There are three basic ways that we can learn to discern God's voice: First, we should be aware that God will speak to us spontaneously. Have you ever been driving down the road and had a thought come to you to pray for a certain person? Did you believe that it was God telling you to pray? Was it an audible voice, or was it a spontaneous thought that came upon your mind? If we become more aware of these instances in our lives, we find that we are experiencing "spirit-level" communication. Scripture confirms this kind of communication. For example, *paga,* a Hebrew word for intercession, is "a chance encounter or an accidental intersecting." When God lays a burden on our heart, He does it through *paga*—a "chance-encounter" thought which "accidentally" intersects our minds. So, when you want to hear from God, be aware of the "chance-encounters" or "spontaneous thoughts."

Second, we must learn to "be still," so that we are able to more readily hear God's voice. God's voice is what we hear in the quietness. In this world there is only noise. It is interesting that stillness is defined as "muted." Many times, when we're yearning to hear from God, we're doing all the talking and not doing enough listening. To receive a pure Word from God, it is very important that your heart be properly focused. If you fix your eyes upon Jesus, the intuitive flow comes from Jesus. But, if you fix your gaze upon some desire of your heart, the intuitive flow comes out of that desire. To have a pure flow, you must become still and carefully fix your eyes upon Jesus. It's a quiet worship.

> *Does God care?*
> *Yes, He sent Jesus to give you peace*
> *and victory over all of your storms of life*
> *through your faith in Him. You see,*
> *He made the choice to die,*
> *so that He would never*
> *have to live without you.*

Let us fix our eyes on Jesus, the author and perfecter of our faith, who for the joy set before him endured the cross, scorning its shame, and sat down at the right hand of the throne of God. (Hebrews 12:2 NIV)

We must become quiet in His presence and share with Him what is on our heart. As you continually enter into His presence, spontaneous thoughts will more readily flow from the throne of God into your heart and soul.

Third, we should journal our prayers *and* God's answers. God told Habakkuk to record the vision (Hab. 2:2). The Scriptures have many examples of individuals' prayers and God's replies (Psalms, many of the prophets, Revelation). Everything that we encounter in our time spent with God must be tested against His Word. When you journal your faith, you're thwarting the ability of doubt to intersect and discount your encounter with God. Before long, you'll find yourself communicating with the living God; yearning for Him more and more.

Knowing God through the Bible is the foundation to hearing His voice. So, you must have a solid commitment to know and obey His Word. You must continually seek Him, so that you are not overcome by the "noise" of the storm. When we allow ourselves to be overcome by the "noise" of this world, we open a door that leads to endless spiritual battles; our enemy uses the "noise" to his advantage.

Be careful! Watch out for attacks from the Devil,
your great enemy. He prowls around like a roaring lion,
looking for some victim to devour.
Take a firm stand against him, and be strong in your faith.
Remember that your Christian brothers and sisters
all over the world are going through the same
kind of suffering you are.
(1 Peter 5:8-9 NLT)

But God has given us our weapon,

And you will know the truth
and the truth will set you free.
(John 8:32 NLT)

Yes, the Truth. Jesus died, not so that we might continue to be defeated and overcome by our storms, but that we might have victory *through* them. Does God care? . . . Yes, He sent Jesus to give you peace and victory over all of your storms of life through your faith in Him. We are to declare the victory in Jesus' name. The victory is yours. The current battle you are in has already been won. The storm you are in right now has been overcome. Victory over all of your storms of life is there for the taking. It brings Jesus great sorrow when we do not allow His death and resurrection to represent victory in each and every one of our lives.

You see, the enemy doesn't want to hear about the blood that was shed for us. Satan doesn't want to hear about sins being forgiven. Satan doesn't want you to know that your storm can be calmed. Satan wants you believing that God doesn't care. Satan will *flood* your life with a million lies each and every day, in an attempt to convince you that you are going to drown and he has won. His goal is simple: to destroy your faith in God.

We must hold on to every Word of God, in order to make it through this journey. We must hold on to what is true . . . it is God's Word, His Promises.

Turn my eyes from worthless things,
and give me life through your word.
(Psalm 119:37 NLT)

Such things were written in the Scriptures long ago to teach us. They give us hope and encouragement as we wait patiently for God's promises. (Romans 15:4 NLT)

But Jesus told him, "No! The Scriptures say, people need more than bread for their life; they must feed on every word of God." (Matthew 4:4 NLT)

God sent Jesus to remind us of the Promises that He made to us and then He gave us new life! God knew, since the fall of man, our sins could never be repaid and that we would have to contend with the fleshly ways of this world. Yes, we must do battle and *there will be raging storms*; but, we can claim the victory through them all, knowing that Jesus Christ is our Lord and Savior.

The Scriptures reveal exactly what power God's Word has in our life; to the measure we use it, it is manifested in our life.

*Then He said to them,
"Take heed what you hear.
With the same measure you use it,
it will be measured to you;
and to you who hear,
more will be given."*
(Mark 4:24 NKJV)

The more time we spend in the Word, the better understanding we will have of God's ways. In grasping the Truth through His Word, we are better equipped to receive the promises that He has made to us as believers. You can only receive the Promises if you know what you should be expecting. In order to make it through our storms, we must cling to Truth and . . .

"Be Still."

God Speaks in the Storm

When we're diligently seeking God and longing to hear from Him, we'll find ourselves in more spiritual battles than we ever thought possible. Meditating on His Word will help us win the daily battles we must face. And yes, it's a minute by minute, hour by hour, day by day, week by week, and year after year battle. The enemy doesn't quit. If we win a battle, he waits quietly until the next opportunity comes along.

> *When the devil had finished temping Jesus,*
> *he left him until the next opportunity came.*
> (Luke 4:13 NLT)

Satan's lies never stop. Many times, just as we're on the verge of a breakthrough, Satan unleashes a relentless attack. He knows our blessing is on the way and he'll do anything to stop it. He'll conveniently provide what seems like "answers" or "solutions." He'll show you a "quick" escape. He'll convince you that his way is the only way to make it out of the storm without all the pain and suffering. He'll *assure* you that you don't need God. He'll persuade you into thinking that you can "save yourself." He'll promise you the desires of your heart, and *he'll make the lies believable.*

But I am not surprised!
Even Satan can disguise himself as an angel of light.
(2 Corinthians 11:14 NLT)

Make no mistake about it . . . Satan is in this for the long haul. He has great patience and incredible persistence. But, God laughs, and so should we, because we've read the end of the Book! We know how it all ends! God has the victory! Therefore, since Christ is in us, we too have the victory!

For this is the secret: Christ lives in you,
and this is your assurance that you
will share in his glory.
(Colossians 1:27 NLT)

At times, it's a real struggle to hear from God. We wonder, "If Satan is so deceitful, how can we distinguish what is from God and what is not?" The answer is simple . . . we can find Him guiding and directing us through His Word. As we're feeling injustice reign in our lives and we're being asked to trust in a Book, we can dig deeper in our faith to find that nothing has been more tested and tried than the Word of God. We can count on God's faithfulness.

As for God, His way is perfect!
The word of the Lord is tested and *tried;*
He is a shield to all those who take refuge
and put their trust in Him.
(Psalm 18:30 AMP)

> *Your promises have been thoroughly tested;*
> *that is why I love them so much.*
> (Psalm 119:140 NLT)

> *The LORD's promises are pure,*
> *like silver refined in a furnace,*
> *purified seven times over.*
> (Psalm 12:6 NLT)

Maybe you're not sure God wants to speak to *you*, or maybe you're not certain that through your sin you will be able to hear Him. Rest assured, if God wants to speak to you . . . He will. So, if you haven't been walking with God, be certain that God is able to reveal Himself even to those who don't "know" Him and have never heard His voice.

Now Samuel did not yet know the Lord:
The word of the Lord had not yet been revealed to him.
(1 Samuel 3:7 NIV)

The Lord came and stood there, calling as at other times, "Samuel! Samuel!" Then Samuel said, "Speak, for your servant is listening." (1 Samuel 3:10 NIV)

God knows that we can come to "know" His voice if we will open our hearts and embrace His Word. God's Word continually reminds us that we can hear His voice; we should have no doubt that we can...

if we listen.

My sheep recognize my voice;
I know them, and they follow me.
(John 10:27 NLT)

It should be no surprise that God speaks to us in the quietness. This is *prime time* for God. Maybe you're like so many who are afraid to experience "aloneness." Maybe you feel like you always have to have some kind of constant noise in your life: a radio, TV, cell phone, computer, or a relationship. It's when we're faced with heavy silence that we find ourselves in God's presence.

It's in those moments that we begin to feel *fear*. Why fear? It's because, many times, it's in the quietness that God *convicts* us. It's in the silence that He calls us to follow Him. We're constantly drowning Him out . . . whether we realize it or not. It is in "being still" that God is able to have time alone with you, in order to speak to your heart without all of the interference. It is in the quietness and stillness that you

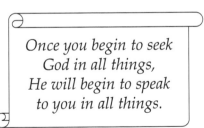

Once you begin to seek God in all things, He will begin to speak to you in all things.

will feel His presence and hear His voice. When your soul is quieted, you are able to *truly* feel His presence; in that moment you will know, without a doubt, that He cares for you more than you can imagine.

The key to hearing God is opening our hearts and minds to whatever His voice might say. We must accept whatever God's voice convicts us of in our lives. We must not only be willing to listen, but we must be willing to follow His instructions. When God tells us to stop bailing water from the boat . . . it would be quite *arrogant and ignorant* to continue bailing. If He tells us to start rowing, it would be foolish to just sit there and remain in the middle of a violent storm! We must show reverence and obedience. We MUST do what God says. He's with us to guide us through the storm . . . He's taking us somewhere. When you're trusting in Christ, you're assured of the *destination* . . . it's the *journey* that matters. And God knows that in this journey, we long for peace.

When the storm rages and you don't know which way to go, or if He cares, you should know that when God speaks, there is only peace.

> *And let the peace*
> *[soul harmony which comes]*
> *from Christ rule*
> *[act as umpire continually] in your hearts*
> *[deciding and settling with all finality*
> *all questions that arise in your minds].*
> (Colossians 3:14 AMP)

When God directs you, there is conviction in your heart and complete peace about the direction of the situation. This is God's voice: direct, brief, and strong. *Once you begin to seek God in all things, He will begin to speak to you in all things.*

God Knows What He's Doing

We can be tempted to believe that God doesn't have a handle on our situation . . . it seems that way, as everything goes spiraling out of control. If we're experiencing a hurricane in life, it's difficult to see how we'll survive . . . much less imagine finding anything left after all the destruction. But, God always has a plan in the storm.

> *It is in and through your storms that He desires to do something awesome in and through YOU! God will use your storms of life — you can be certain of it. God wastes nothing!*

When Jesus looked up and saw a great crowd coming toward him, he said to Philip, "Where shall we buy bread for these people to eat?" **He asked this only to test him, for he already had in mind what he was going to do.** (John 6:5-6 NIV)

The storm on the Sea of Galilee was a test. *Jesus knew there would be a storm. He knows about every storm in your life, too.* He knows exactly what *He's* going to do . . . He's more interested in what *you're* going to do. God doesn't tempt you, but He tests you . . . *in order to grow you.* You see, sometimes we bring storms on ourselves through sin, poor judgment, or just a lack of experience; some storms may come by the wrongdoing of other people. If Satan brings a storm, we can be certain it is to draw us away from God and destroy our faith. But *if God brings a storm, He brings it with great purposes.* No matter how the storm is brought about, God will use it. You can be certain . . . God wastes nothing.

It is in and through our storms that He desires to do something awesome in and through us. He uses the storms to get our attention. He wants us to know that He is concerned about *everything* in our lives. He wants us to learn to place our trust in Him through all of our storms in life. *He wants our faith directed at Him and nothing else.*

We do not know what to do, but our eyes are upon you. (2 Chronicles 20:12 NIV)

My eyes are ever on the Lord . . . (Psalm 25:15 NIV)

Once our eyes are upon Him, He convicts us and uses the storm to purify us from sin. Through the storms, God calls attention to those areas that are not pleasing to Him. He shows us the good, the bad, and the ugly; He convicts us, yet doesn't condemn us.

You can be certain that if God reveals areas of your life that need to be thrown overboard, *He* will empower you to do what He's asking you to do. He's not asking you to do it in your own strength, but in His. And don't be deceived, it will take constant effort. *You will fail,* and you will need to *continually* go to the foot of the Cross.

God is using the storms of our lives to bring us to a place of *complete* surrender; for God, it's an all or nothing deal. So, don't try and surrender some things and hoard others. You can't have one foot in heaven's door and one foot in the world (1 John 2:15). The storms of our lives bring us to a place of making decisions. Will we trust God? Will we follow Him? Or will we run the other direction in fear? If you will face the fear in your circumstances with your faith, you'll be amazed at the miracles that God will work in your life.

> *If you'll make the decision to face the fear in your circumstances with your faith, you'll stand amazed at the miracles God will work in your life.*

We have choices in our storms. Will we cast blame and become resentful and bitter, or will we turn to God and ask, "What is Your purpose?" Surrender is what God is after in *your* life. He wants *all* of you. He loves you that much. His miracle in your storm is that you can rest with Him. Our lives begin to change dramatically when we enter into His rest. God will not compete with us. He will allow us to go "our way," until we choose His. His desire is for us to acknowledge His sovereignty in our lives. But, we can only enter into His rest, ceasing our drifting and finding stability and security through our storms, when we grab hold of our "*Anchor.*"

I cry out to the Lord; I plead for the Lord's mercy. I pour out my complaints before him and tell him all my troubles. For I am overwhelmed, and you alone know the way I should turn. (Psalm 142:1-3 NLT)

The Lord hears his people when they call to him for help. He rescues them from all their troubles. The Lord is close to the brokenhearted; he rescues those who are crushed in spirit. (Psalm 34:17-18 NLT)

Yes, everything else is worthless when compared with the priceless gain of knowing Christ Jesus my Lord. I have discarded everything else, counting it all as garbage, so that I may have Christ and become one with him. I no longer count on my own goodness or my ability to obey God's law, but I trust Christ to save me.
(Philippians 3: 8-9 NLT)

Search for the Lord and for his strength, and keep on searching. (Psalm 105: 4 NLT)

I am blessed because I seek refuge and put my trust in the Lord." (Psalm 2:12 NLT)

But as for me, I will always have hope; I will praise you more and more. (Psalm 71:14 NIV)

They cried out to the Lord in their trouble, and he delivered them from their distress. (Psalm 107:6 NIV)

Get away from me, Satan! You are a dangerous trap to me. You are seeing things merely from a human point of view, and not from God's. (Matthew 16:23 NLT)

I command you- be strong and courageous! Do not be afraid or discouraged. For the Lord your God is with you wherever you go. (Joshua 1:9 NLT)

So, you see, it is impossible to please God without faith. Anyone who wants to come to him must believe that there is a God and that he rewards those who sincerely seek him. (Hebrews 11:6 NLT)

I look up to the mountains-does my help come from there? My help comes from the Lord, who made the heavens and the earth!" (Psalm 121: 1-2 NLT)

Who among you fears the Lord and obeys his servant? If you are walking in darkness, without a ray of light, trust in the Lord and rely on your God. (Isaiah 50:10 NLT)

The Lord will work out his plans for my life-for your faithful love, O Lord, endures forever. Don't abandon me, for you made me. (Psalm 138:8 NLT)

Be glad for all God is planning for you. Be patient in trouble, and always be prayerful. (Romans 12:12 NLT)

So if you are suffering according to God's will, keep on doing what is right, and trust yourself to the God who made you, for he will never fail you. (1 Peter 4:19 NLT)

But the Lord waits for you to come to him so he can show you his love and compassion. For the Lord is a faithful God. Blessed are those who wait for him to help them. (Isaiah 30:18 NLT)

The Lord is near to all who call on him, to all who call on him in truth. He fulfills the desires of those who fear him; he hears their cry and saves them. The Lord watches over all who love him, but all the wicked he will destroy. (Psalm 145:18-20 NIV)

Be merciful to me, O God, be merciful to me! For my soul trusts in You; and in the shadow of Your wings I will make my refuge, until these calamities have passed by. I will cry out to God Most High, to God who performs all things for me. He shall send from heaven and save me; He reproached the one who would swallow me up. God shall send forth his mercy and his truth. (Psalm 57:1-3 NLT)

Mightier than the thunder of the great waters, mightier than the breakers in the sea – the Lord on high is mighty. (Psalm 93:4 NIV)

Chapter 4

⚓ Where is Your Faith? ⚓

In Pursuit of Peace

We have a hard time imagining the peace that Jesus had in the back of the boat. We *long* to have that kind of rest. It's hard to comprehend being in a furious storm, waves capsizing the boat, men screaming for their lives, and Jesus . . . *asleep*.

> *Wake up O Lord! Why do you sleep? Get up!*
> *Do not reject us forever. Why do you look the other way?*
> *Why do you ignore our suffering and oppression? Rise up!*
> *Help us! Ransom us because of your unfailing love.*
> (Psalm 44:23, 24, 26)

We wonder how He could possibly sleep through it all; yet we have all felt so exhausted, at one time or another, from bailing water out of our boat that we, too, have felt that we could sleep through just about anything. In fact, we'd love to just say, *"Wake me up when it's all over!"*

But, what if you could have *true peace* and *rest* during the most violent storms of your life? Guess

what? *You can.* Jesus came not only to give us the
way of salvation, but He also left us a gift. It's a gift
that is ours forever . . . when we accept Christ as
Lord and Savior—He fills us with the Holy Spirit
who enables us to have peace of mind and heart.

> *Our peace will always depend upon the
> resignation of our lives into God's hands,
> regardless of our circumstances.
> If we release our hold on our lives,
> God will empower us to endure any hardship.*

*I am leaving you with a gift — peace of mind and heart.
And the peace I give isn't like the peace the world gives.
So don't be troubled or afraid.*
(John 14:27 NLT)

What Jesus offers us can only come from totally
resigning ourselves into the hands of God. It means
completely surrendering and putting ourselves under His power, wisdom, and mercy. It means being
led according to *His* will. Our peace will always *depend* upon the resignation of our lives into God's
hands, *regardless of our circumstances.* If we will re-
lease the hold we have on our lives, God will empower us to endure any hardship. He wants us to go
about life "as usual" and live in confidence without
fear or anxiety — *trusting in Him.* You see, the more

resigned you are to God's sovereign care, the more indifferent you'll be to the raging storm around you. You won't be concerned about the future; you won't be constantly trying to figure out the next step because you have entrusted your life into the loving hands of Almighty God.

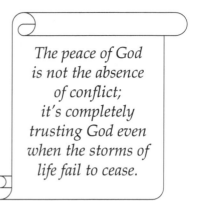

The peace of God is not the absence of conflict; it's completely trusting God even when the storms of life fail to cease.

The peace that Jesus offers is like an "Anchor" for our souls. When we're trusting in God, we can surrender all of our doubts and fears to Him. We can entrust every storm into His care. We can trust in Him because He *promises* we can. It may not be easy, we may still have to go through pain and suffering, but God has promised to never leave us nor forsake us. It has been said,

> *"Faith doesn't make things easy,*
> *but it makes all things possible."*

In the back of the boat, Jesus was teaching us that there is *nothing* to fear. God is with us always. He doesn't offer the peace that the world gives . . . He offers a *much different* kind of peace. The peace of this world is based on a *feeling*. His peace comes from *faith*. We usually base our peace and joy on the state of our circumstances; we've determined that we'll have peace "when . . ."

Too often, we have expectations for our lives, and when those expectations are met . . . *then* we decide we can have peace. We demand control. It's a vicious cycle of trying to take control, change things, and make *something* happen! We're constantly trying to do things that *only God can do*. It's our lack of ability to control it all that steals our peace. This is why Jesus made it clear: The peace He was giving us was *"His peace."*

> *If you find yourself drifting in the current,*
> *if you've ventured off course by way of the raging*
> *wind and waves, drop your Anchor down . . .*
> *let go of your fear by grabbing*
> *hold of your faith.*

His peace isn't hinged on whether or not there's a storm in our life at the moment. His peace is secured when we are "one" with Him. Peace is not the absence of conflict — it's completely trusting God even when the storms of life fail to cease. When it all comes down to it, our problem doesn't lie within the storm . . . *it lies within us*. Our struggles go far beyond the circumstances in our storm — our problem is with God. When the storms of life are raging, we become upset, angry, and emotionally distraught; everything in our lives is colored by our emotional state. It's impossible for the storm to be calmed, until we find peace with God; *it starts with inviting Him into the boat with you.* He IS our peace:

For he himself is our peace . . . (Ephesians 2:14 NIV)

Once we've made the decision to ask Jesus to get into the boat with us, once we've settled our hearts in knowing that He is there, when we've placed our lives in His hands, and we see Him with us, we can begin to see our storms of life from a completely different perspective. What we find is that as we step out in faith and we're in a boat with Jesus, we can ride out some of the most treacherous storms imaginable. Our faith will always take us further than we believe we can go, *when we have peace with God.*

> *Our faith will always take us further,*
> *in the storms of our lives,*
> *than we believe we can go . . .*
> *when we have peace with God.*

In this storm, on the Sea of Galilee, Jesus is showing us many things, but the underlying, powerful message was to teach us how our faith will overcome our fear. You see, once we've directed our attention to God . . . He can begin to work. Once we've refocused our faith, when we've turned our situation over to Him and relinquished control over it all, God shows us something amazing: He shows us how to rest in Him through our faith. Jesus is our "Anchor." He is the Living Word. It's our "Anchor" that gives us stability and security through the most violent storms of our lives. If you find yourself drifting in the current or if you've ventured off course by way of the raging winds and waves...drop your *Anchor* down . . . *let go of your fear by grabbing hold of your faith.*

Faith to Calm the Storm

Fear—it strikes without warning and won't let go, until we face it. Throughout the Bible, "Do not fear," is the resounding message. We don't have to contemplate, very long, why this message was so vital ... God knows that *fear destroys our faith*. Fear dissolves in the face of our faith in Almighty God who protects us, strengthens us, and gives us victory through every storm of life. Faith cannot exist with fear and vice versa. We must *choose* faith *or* fear—it's a decision. God empowers us through His Word to have confidence in Him and choose faith.

I call heaven and earth to witness this day against you
that I have set before you life and death,
the blessings and the curses; therefore choose life,
that you and your descendants may live.
(Deuteronomy 30:19 AMP)

The enemy of faith is fear . . . which is often accompanied by doubt and unbelief. It's sometimes difficult to understand what comes first...the doubt and unbelief, or fear. It's a "chicken or the egg" scenario. Quite frankly, it doesn't really make a difference . . . either way, we continually get eggs . . . *and we continually face fear.*

As difficult as it might be for us to acknowledge, unbelief in God is a sin. That's hard for most of us to come to grips with . . . we must face the fact that we *continually* sin. It's when we throw ourselves at the foot of the Cross that we find God's limitless power and boundless grace. God always makes a way. It's our faith that overcomes all the doubt and unbelief.

You see, doubt and unbelief are motivated by pride, rebellion, and often times, ignorance. If we are using our "Anchor," then we're diving into God's Word and absorbing the Truth that is in it. If we're consuming the Word, then it will convict us and move us forward in our faith.

For the word of God is living and active.
Sharper than any double-edged sword,
it penetrates even to dividing soul and spirit,
joints and marrow; it judges the thoughts
and attitudes of the heart.
(Hebrews 4:12 NIV)

It's our doubt that breeds discouragement, and we can find ourselves in an endless cycle of believing God . . . *only when He shows up*. But God doesn't work that way. He says, "Believe," *then* you'll see. We can't get to the back of the boat, and the storms of our lives will never be calmed, without faith in the One who calms them.

God doesn't always part Red Seas. He doesn't always speak from a burning bush. He doesn't always heal the sick. And *He doesn't always calm the storm*. So, our faith can't depend upon it. Our faith must simply believe that God is sovereign, merciful, and gracious; faith trusts that God's ways are *always* best. Sometimes, it means He allows a raging storm that brings pain and suffering. Faith believes He does it for our good, even though we can't understand it. Faith in God will bring you greater joy than you can ever imagine, if you will rely on His strength and presence to help you endure.

> *We can't get to the back of the boat and the storms of our lives will never be calmed without faith in the One who calms them.*

Faith in God gave Jesus enough peace to rest during a raging storm on the Sea. Faith in God can give you peace, as you frantically struggle to make it through your storm, too. We should never forget, as we journey through every storm, *it is God who allows the storms to come.* If He's allowed it . . . He's found purpose in it.

> *Our storms are inevitable, but our "Anchor,"*
> *(Jesus) the Living Word, is immovable.*
> *When your faith is in God, you can experience*
> *stability and security through*
> *every raging storm of life.*

The Bible makes this Truth, abundantly, clear through the lives of Job and Peter: It is through the express permission of the Heavenly Father that our tests of faith come. Satan cannot test the faith of any child of God without the Lord's permission. (Never forget: God has a *purpose* AND a *plan* in every storm that comes into our lives.) When Jesus delivered his warning to Peter before the crucifixion, Jesus encouraged Peter by saying, *"But I have prayed for you, that your faith may not fail"* (Luke 22:32 NIV). Clearly, Jesus knew that Peter would come through his trials with his faith intact. Jesus' words imply that He had a specific plan for Peter's life through many severe trials he was about to face. He wanted Peter to remember, in his time of despair, he was to fight the fight of faith; the same is true for us in our storms of life. God has a plan to use every one of our storms in life, and He has prayed that our faith will not fail!

Faith in God can calm the storms of our lives. It's interesting to note the fact: In the midst of a life threatening storm, Jesus didn't even address the Disciples' "fear" . . . He cut right to the heart of it all, by simply asking, *"Where is your faith"* (Luke 8:25 NLT)? So, you must ask *yourself, "Where is my faith?"* Are you looking at your storm, or are you looking to your God? As we face the raging sea that's threatening to take us under, it's difficult, at best, to see where we are or where we're going; but, faith knows that the miracle of its calming has already been arranged. Faith is reaching for God's hand, knowing He is there, even when we can't see Him. You can rest assured that He's *never* out of reach—He's *much closer* than you think. When the wind and rain blinds you and it becomes difficult to even breathe, faith knows that God will answer you out of the storm in *His* way . . . in *His* timing.

> *Then the Lord answered Job out of the storm.*
> (Job 38:1 NIV)

> *One thing you can be sure of,*
> *God is never out of reach —*
> *He's much closer than you think.*

The Purpose of Faith

Faith in God makes all things possible because faith in God calls upon supernatural power that has *no boundaries*. Our greatest moment in a storm of life can come when we're at wit's end, and we realize that nothing short of a miracle will help us through the storm. In the face of uncertainty, we can turn to God and He can calm the storm that rages within us . . . in the blink of an eye. That's what He does . . . He is *truly* amazing. As an omnipotent, omniscient, and loving God, He gives us a miracle *in* the storm that we would have never otherwise experienced . . . had He not allowed the storm in the first place. When we're looking back on our storms of life, had God not allowed them, we would never meet the one true God, never witness His miraculous provision and power, and we'd never learn to fully trust Him. It's our trust in Him that brings true peace throughout the journey — the peace Jesus came to give us.

Storms are inevitable, but our anchor is *immovable*. If we're standing upon our faith in Jesus, the Living Word, then we can experience a stability and security which is not easily humanly understood.

When the storms of life come,
the wicked are whirled away,
but the godly have a lasting foundation.
(Proverbs 10:24-25 NLT)

When we're trusting in God's Promises, His Truth will blow away all the distractions that keep us from being focused upon Him. Most of the time, we don't know when our storms are coming, but God knows; we can trust in Him to take us *through* them, if necessary.

As we trust, we will find ourselves in the peak of the storm, and we can often find ourselves overcome by a "Rogue Wave." When these waves hit, we're quite certain that all hope is gone. A Rogue Wave creates a vertical wall of water that is proceeded by a trough, so deep, that it is referred to as a "hole in the sea"; *A Rogue Wave in your life can develop a hole in your heart . . . when fear consumes your faith.*

At times, researchers have found these waves to reach over 110ft. They can appear from nowhere, without warning; they usually move against the prevailing current and wave direction, and they can often occur in perfectly clear weather. The Rogue Waves in our lives are no different. As we take a step of faith, venturing into the depths with Jesus, we can face the threat of sinking in our boat . . . within a matter of minutes.

Know this: If you've encountered a Rogue Wave in your life . . . you're actually moving in the right direction. When a Rogue Wave is formed, it's because strong winds from a storm are blowing in the opposite direction of the ocean, and it's the strong current forces that randomly generate the Rogue

Waves. Here's how it applies to your storm of life: When you take steps of faith, when you're traveling in a boat with Jesus, when you're trusting in God, you're going against the "direction" the world wants to take you. When you've decided to live your life according to God's will, you have rejected your enemy, and it creates a strong oppositional force . . . *don't be surprised by Rogue Waves* . . . they're just part of the journey in the sea of life . . . when you're traveling with Jesus.

It's when things get worse, instead of better, all hope seems gone, and we must ultimately make the choice as to whether the storm will *destroy us* or *develop us*. In our storms of life, it is our *response* that is the key. The begging question haunts us, *"Where is your faith?"*

We can easily become discouraged, as guilt overwhelms us, when we realize that our faith is lacking; we're not sure how we could possibly display more faith than we already have. But, there are times when we are so busy trying to have faith and seek God's direction that we look right past Him and the work He is already doing in our storm. Our faith is just as lacking as the Disciples' in the boat.

The Disciples were in a raging storm with Jesus, yet they looked right past the fact that it was the Son of God that was in the boat with them! It wasn't until the point that they were about to drown that they suddenly cried out to Jesus for help! Not only did they wait until the last minute, but they cried out in bitterness, *"Lord, don't you care?"*

We can easily be overwhelmed with despair, as the waves are crashing down upon us. We're crying out to God and begging for mercy, but we're only met with *silence*. Prayers go unanswered, and the anger within us grows deeper. Our soul begs the question, *"Where is God?"*

The problem is that we tend to place limitations on God. We decide *when* and *where* He should show up. We decide *how* and *what* He'll do in our situation. We're looking for a mighty roar from a mountaintop...with lightning bolts and parting clouds—we miss His whisper of eternal hope through His Word. We only seem to recognize Him when He's "walking on the water" . . . *or do we?*

Walking on Water

You'd think that the miracle of Jesus calming the storm on the Sea of Galilee would be enough to secure the Disciples' faith in Jesus. But, just like us, the Disciples had a short memory. God examined their hearts along their journey with Jesus and realized, believe it or not, that they needed to be tested in this area of their lives, *once more.*

How many times have we felt like we've been tested in an area of our lives over and over again? We find ourselves experiencing "déjà vu" moments, and wonder why? (Remember, God knows what He's doing, He's always at work, and He's constantly perfecting our faith.) In the Sea of Galilee, somehow, they missed it . . . *they didn't get the message* . . . so God had to send a "different" storm in their journey.

This time, Jesus tells his Disciples to get in a boat *without* Him. He sends them out alone, deliberately, and then He goes up into the hills to pray. All too often, we see this scenario in our own lives: A storm comes, overwhelms us, and we're faced with the *seeming absence* of Jesus. But, we forget: *He's up on the hillside praying for us.*

Often times, it's when we're at wit's end, God steps in and brings about a miracle – when it will have its most dramatic impact. Never forget: God knows what He's doing!

We so easily overlook what God has shown us; we forget the miracles that He has previously done in our lives . . . *so did the Disciples.* You see, they had already seen Jesus calm the storm (though He was physically in the boat with them), they had seen Him heal and raise the dead to life, and they had just seen Him feed the five thousand. He had sent them out and given them His power; they had seen their ministry confirmed by the hand of God working through them. But, somehow, they just "missed it." Seems they didn't quite get it . . . *and when we don't "get it,"* it's necessary that God tests us as many times as it requires . . . so that we *will* "get it!"

It was after the storm had blown for several hours and the Disciples were in deep distress that Jesus came to them — *walking upon the water*. Once again, waiting until they were at "wit's end," Jesus steps in. And He does it not one moment before that point. He acted upon God's perfect timing. Amazingly, as He walks toward the boat, the Disciples think he's a ghost! They don't even recognize Him!

We're no different, in that we fail to see Jesus with us in the storms of our lives. Even when He comes *walking on the water* . . . we fail to recognize Him. We trust Jesus for salvation and the forgiveness of sins, we look to Him as the supplier of all our needs, and we trust Him to bring us into eternity one day, but when a sudden storm falls upon us and it seems as though our world is falling apart, we find it difficult to see Jesus — *we fail to recognize Him in the storm*. When things *really* get rough . . . we're just not sure He's there. This time, however, Jesus addresses the heart of the issue — *fear*.

But Jesus spoke to them at once. "Don't be afraid," he said. "Take courage! I am here!" Then he climbed into the boat, and the wind stopped. They were totally amazed, . . .
(Mark 6:50, 51 NLT)

We find the Disciples, walking out their faith, following Jesus, and *being faced with a lack of faith.* In this particular test, which they had been trained on in the Sea of Galilee, they failed. They got nothing but an "F" — their *faith failed* as a result of their *fear.* Again, they wondered to themselves, "Who is this?" We so quickly pass judgment on their faith, but *we* continually fail the same test.

God has rescued us many times before; yet, when we've been walking in faith and suddenly a storm comes along, *our faith fails.* We ask, *"Who is this?"* Who sends or allows the raging storms into our lives? Who tests us? Who provides for our every need and then tests us on it? Who gives us Promises and then sends us out to see if we believe what we teach or what we say? Who? *It is God Himself.* He is training us just as He was training the Disciples. He's building our faith, so that we

> *As we travel along the troubled seas of our lives, faith rises to the occasion and trusts God even if He doesn't present us with a burning bush, even if He doesn't walk to us on the water, and even if He doesn't calm the storm — faith keeps on trusting Him and remains at peace through it all.*

can be confident and calm—able to cope and endure the storms of our lives. There was a simple lesson through these storms...not some deep and mysterious one. He simply wanted the Disciples, and us, to maintain peace and confident hope in life's darkest hours. That's it! *All* He wants is your faith!

> *All God wants*
> *is your faith.*
> *That's it!*

As we travel along the troubled seas of our lives, faith rises to the occasion and trusts God even if He doesn't present us with a burning bush, even if He doesn't walk to us on the water, even if He doesn't calm the storm—faith keeps on trusting Him and remains at peace through it all.

We tend to cling to a faith that believes . . . "if." If God does "this" . . . "*then*" *I'll believe*. If God puts a burning bush in front of me and speaks, *then I'll believe.* Maybe you're not *that* demanding, but your faith is hinged on Him proving himself in some marvelous, manifested way. "*If God comes through in my time frame, then I'll have greater trust."* We open a door for the enemy; before we know it, the winds and waves begin to pick up and the storm intensifies.

Doesn't God hear the cries for help? We demand that He do something and anxiously wonder what He's going to do and when He's going to do it . . . *all the while He's looking to us . . . wondering what we will do.* Will we continue the journey in fear, or will we rest in Him?

> *We wonder if God hears us and what He's going to do. All the while, He's looking to us . . . wondering what we will do. Will we continue the journey in fear or will we trust in Him?*

As we wrestle with our faith, we find that God is allowing us to be brought to our knees so that there is nothing left for us to do, but look up. If we turn to Him, trusting in Him in the midst of all the adversity, He is faithful and just. Faith in God accepts what appears unreasonable and believes that God knows its reason. We may not realize it, but our soul longs for greater faith because we know that faith in God makes the impossible...*possible*. Faith in God allows us to see the unseen, believe the unbelievable, and experience the miracles that He longs to give us. Faith is the key!

So that's why faith is the key! (Romans 5:16 NLT)

Don't be confused, faith is *not* hope. Faith is not a "positive desire." Faith is not simply, "knowing" the

Word. (Many professing Christians "mentally" believe that the Bible is the Word of God, but their belief doesn't change the way they live.) Faith is not a way to manipulate God. It's not some magical power by which we make God do what WE want, when He would otherwise be unwilling to do it. Listen, even demons believe in God!

You believe that there is one God. Good!
Even the demons believe that — and shudder.
(James 2:19 NIV)

Faith is an unwavering confidence in God—it's moving ahead, bold and confident, with patience in knowing that God's help is on the way. It's trusting that He *will* show up in His perfect way and at the perfect time.

> *The kind of faith that "saves," responds to God's*
> *Promises by taking a step forward into the*
> *unknown — trusting God completely.*
> *It's a faith that is manifested in the heart*
> *before it ever sees the evidence.*

We might be convinced that we're *full* of faith, when we're really just full of hope — anxiously looking for results. We lack the settled confidence and assurance that faith has. Faith in God is having the kind of trust and confidence in Christ that leads you to "follow Him." And as we've discovered, sometimes that means getting into a boat and heading right into a raging storm.

Although we may feel that we're taking a blind step of faith into an uncertain future, with each successive step that we take, we will experience God's faithfulness and we'll develop the faith that learns to trust God, regardless of what we "see." *This is the kind of faith that saves.* It's faith that responds to God's Promises and moves forward. Faith causes you to know in your heart before you see with your eyes:

> *For we live by believing and not by seeing*
> (2 Corinthians 5:7 NLT)

You don't need a faith that is based upon religious ideas and doctrines or traditions. You desperately need "*saving faith.*" Saving faith comes from one place and one place only . . . Jesus, the Living Word. The faith that you find through Jesus is the faith that brings salvation (Ephesians 2:8, 9; John 3:16; John 5:24). It's the faith that saves you and brings about God's deliverance in all circumstances.

Saving faith always has corresponding actions . . . it means acting according to what you believe. To live by faith means to walk forward with confidence in God *without doubting*. You can't "*try*" to believe God. *You either believe Him or you don't.* We have to stop "trying" and simply start "*trusting . . .*" if we want to have the kind of faith that saves us in our storms.

What good is it, dear brothers and sisters, if you say you have faith but don't show it by your actions? Can that kind of faith save anyone? (James 2:14 NLT)

Help My Unbelief!

Too often, when we examine our faith, we're faced with the truth that our faith is lacking. We, coming in faith, just like the man who desperately wanted Jesus to heal his demon possessed son, find Jesus saying,

> *"If I can? Anything is possible*
> *if a person believes."* (Mark 9:23 NLT)

As we grasp His words, we're consumed with our need for more faith, and we cry out, just as this man did:

> *"I do believe, but help me overcome my unbelief!"*
> (Mark 9:24 NLT)

> *We have to stop "trying" and simply start "trusting . . ." if we want to have the kind of faith that saves us in our storms of life.*

So, how do we get more faith? How can we have faith that saves us and calms our storms? Jesus taught us that faith comes from God's Word. It comes from trusting in what He says and being confident that He'll do what He says He will do. It comes from hearing *the Good News.*

*Yet faith comes from listening to this message
of good news – the Good News about Christ.*
(Romans 10:17 NLT)

We overcome doubt and disbelief and defeat fear
by applying the Word of God to our lives. There is no
other way. The only way through the storm is to . . .
let down your "Anchor."

*Study this Book of Instruction continually. Meditate on it
day and night so you will be sure to obey everything written in it. Only then will you prosper and succeed in all
you do.* (Joshua 1:8 NLT)

*Turn my eyes away from worthless things; preserve my
life according to your word.* (Psalm 119:37 NLT)

We have this hope as an anchor for the soul, *firm and
secure. It enters the inner sanctuary behind the curtain,
where Jesus, who went before us, has entered on our behalf.
He has become a high priest forever..."*
(Hebrews 6:19-20 NLT)

When we understand God's Word . . . we understand how God thinks. When we learn to think like
God thinks, we can overcome any storm. When we
align our thinking with God's, we're given a glimpse
of what it's like to see through His eyes. When we're

able to view our storm from His perspective . . . *it changes everything.*

After Jesus was baptized, He was led into the wilderness by the Holy Spirit. For forty days and forty nights He went without food and became very hungry. Then the devil showed up. Isn't that just like him? *You know how it is* . . . you're feeling discouraged, beaten down by the raging storm that's been trying to take you under, and just when you think you can't take one more crashing wave . . . one hits.

So, instead of Jesus falling for the many temptations the devil offered, Jesus stood firm. But He stood firm in *one thing* . . . God's Word.

During that time the devil came and said to him, "If you are the Son of God, tell these stones to become loaves of bread." But Jesus told him, "No! The Scriptures say, 'People do not live by bread alone, but by every word that comes from the mouth of God.'"

Then the devil took him to the holy city, Jerusalem, to the highest point of the Temple, and said, "If you are the Son of God, jump off! For the Scriptures say, 'He will order his angels to protect you. And they will hold you up with their hands so you won't even hurt your foot on a stone.'" Jesus responded, "The Scriptures also say, 'You must not test the Lord your God.'" Next the devil took him to the peak of a very high mountain and showed him all the kingdoms of the world and their glory. "I will give it all to you," he said, "if you will kneel down and worship me." "Get out of here, Satan," Jesus told him. "For the Scriptures say, 'You must worship the Lord your God and serve only him.'"

Then the devil went away, and angels came and took care of Jesus. (Matthew 4:1-11 NLT)

He just doesn't stop, but neither does God's Word. The Word of God covers it *all.* Whatever you may be facing, whatever you might be struggling with now or in the future, God has something to say about it. *Don't entertain the devil.* Have faith; act upon it by declaring the Promises of God in the face of doubt, disbelief, and discouragement. *When fear knocks . . . let your faith answer.*

When the devil says to you, "You'll never get that job; there are far more qualified applicants," reply with, *"For I can do everything with the help of Christ who gives me the strength I need!"* (Philippians 4:13 NLT)

When the devil says to you, "You'll never get over your addiction," reply with, *"Greater is He that is in me than he that is in this world."* (1 John 4:4 NLT)

When the devil says to you, "You need to get divorced, your spouse is no good and you deserve better," reply with, *"The Lord God hates divorce!"* (Malachi 2:16 NLT)

When you're told that you must battle a life threatening disease and the devil says, "The end is drawing near," reply with, *". . . prayer offered in faith will heal me . . . the Lord will make me well."*
(James 5:15 NLT)

When you lose your job and the devil laughs at your despair, reply with, *"Taste and see that the Lord is good. Oh, the joy because I trust in him! I will show reverence to*

and honor Him . . . I will have all I need."
(Psalm 34:8-9 NLT)

When your storm of life is threatening to take you
under and you feel you can't hold on any longer,
stand firm in your faith and say, *"I know the Lord is
always with me. I will not be shaken for He is right beside
me!"* (Psalm 16:8 NLT)

It's during our storms that we are confronted
with how well we know God's Word by the amount
of faith that we possess. True faith, the faith that
saves, will only come from believing in God's Promises; it's continually and confidently standing upon
each one.

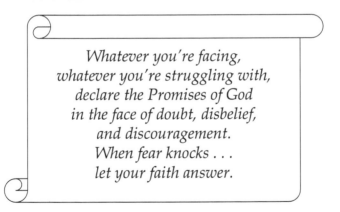

Whatever you're facing,
whatever you're struggling with,
declare the Promises of God
in the face of doubt, disbelief,
and discouragement.
When fear knocks . . .
let your faith answer.

Through God's Promises, we know that we have
the victory — all we need is faith . . . *the size of a mustard seed.* We don't have to have faith that matches
the size of our storm, so we can relax a little. God
doesn't require more of us than what He knows
we're capable of. He's given each of us a measure of
faith and that's all He's going to require of us. He'll

meet us right where we are in our faith.

> *For by the grace given me I say to every one of you:*
> *Do not think of yourself more highly than you ought,*
> *but rather think of yourself with sober judgment,*
> *in accordance with the measure*
> *of faith God has given you.*
> (Romans 12:3 NIV)

You see, "being still" actually requires action—it requires faith. And our faith must be shown by our actions. The question is, *"In your storm, will you just say that you have faith, or will you have faith by showing God that you do?"* You show your faith in God by declaring His Word. He recognizes His own words; He knows what He has spoken, and He is faithful. **God keeps His Word.**

You're Not Alone

Jesus is always with us in our boat because He left us the Holy Spirit. God knew we could not get through the storms of our lives alone.

*If you love me, obey my commandments. And I will ask the Father; and he will give you another Counselor, **who will never leave you.** He is the Holy Spirit, who leads you into all truth.* (John 14; 15-16 NLT)

The Holy Spirit is with us always. If we rely on Him, He will guide us through every situation we face in life. He is there to help us in our distress; when we don't know what to do, when all hope seems gone,

He goes before the Father on our behalf.

And the Holy Spirit helps us in our distress. For we don't even know what we should pray for, nor how we should pray. But the Holy Spirit prays for us with groaning that cannot be expressed by words. And the Father knows all hearts and knows what the Spirit is saying, for the Spirit pleads for us believers in harmony with God's own will. (Romans 8:26 NLT)

How many times have you felt that, as you tried to pray in faith, your pain and sorrow was so deep that you didn't even know HOW to pray? You felt as though nothing you could say or do could truly communicate the needs of your heart. Maybe your pain was so deep that you couldn't even find the energy to pray. Pain and suffering can take the life out of you, if you allow it to. You can become so exhausted from fighting the storm, for so long, that by the time you reach out for God's hand, you're so weak and weary that you simply can't hold on. We've all been there. All of God's children suffer deep anguish that drains the life out of them and causes them to occasionally believe that God has forsaken them.

And at the ninth hour Jesus cried out in a loud voice, "Eloi, Eloi, lama sabachthani?" – which means, "My God, my God, why have you forsaken me?" (Mark 15:34 NLT)

(See Psalm 22—Mark 15:34 is the "question" that is NOT a question. Jesus was referring us to the assurance of Psalm 22 . . . that God's promise to send Christ was fulfilled and that He delivers those who trust in Him.)

You are not forsaken. God asks you in your moment of despair, *"What don't you get? Have you forgotten that I have promised NEVER will I leave you, nor forsake you"* (Hebrews 14:5 NLT)? Each and every storm can be viewed as a trial *or* a testimony to our faith in God.

In your weakest moments, the Holy Spirit is there to help you. You will know that He is at work within you when you start experiencing spiritual growth. You'll begin to have a yearning to know God more than ever before. You won't be satisfied in just knowing God as you know Him now. You will begin to seek Scripture as a lifeline in your storm. You will take every thought captive through the Word of God. You'll become more and more aware of the sin in your life, and you'll come to a place of repentance much more often. As you grow closer to God, you'll begin to understand your desperate need for Him. Those areas of your life that are destructive to your spirit . . . will repulse you. You will continually learn to rely only on God, and you will be convinced that He is the only One who can rescue through your storms of life.

As you grow in your faith, you'll find yourself achieving dreams you never knew you had, overcoming obstacles that seemed insurmountable, and experiencing fulfillment that you couldn't have ever imagined. You'll no longer rely on yourself . . . you'll depend on God's wisdom, guidance, and strength to carry you. Your storms will create a feeling of helplessness and hopelessness, but the Holy Spirit is there to guide you through the storm . . . to strengthen you in the Lord. It is through your faith in God that you will find calm in your storm; it's your faith that enables you to enter into *His rest*.

". . . according to your faith, be it unto you."
(Matthew 9:29 NLT)

For every child of God defeats this evil world by trusting Christ to give the victory. And the ones who win this battle against the world are the ones that believe that Jesus is the Son of God. (1 John 5:4-5 NLT)

What is faith? It is the confident assurance that what we hope for is going to happen. It is the evidence of things we cannot yet see. (Hebrews 11:1 NLT)

For if you carefully obey the law and regulations that the Lord gave to Israel through Moses, you will be successful. Be strong and courageous; do not be afraid or lose heart!
(1 Chronicles 22: 13 NLT)

For whatever is born of God overcomes the world; and this is the victory that has overcome the world-our faith. Who is the one who overcomes the world, but he who believes that Jesus is the Son of God. (1 John 5:4-5 NLT)

You heard their cries for help and saved them.
They put their trust in you and were never disappointed.
(Psalm 22:5 NLT)

You are my refuge and my shield;
I have put my hope in your word. (Psalm 119:114 NIV)

Don't copy the behavior and customs of this world, but let God transform you into a new person by changing the way you think. Then you will know what God wants you to do, and you will know how good and please and perfect his will really is. (Romans 12:2 NLT)

"You didn't have enough faith," Jesus told them. "I assure you, even if you had faith as small as a mustard seed you could say to this mountain, 'Move from here to there,' and it would move. Nothing would be impossible."
(Matthew 17:20 NLT)

For the word of the Lord is right and true;
he is faithful in all He does. (Psalm 33:4 NIV)

Yet he did not waver through unbelief regarding the promise of God, but was strengthened in his faith and gave glory to God, being fully persuaded that God had power to do what he had promised. (Romans 4:20-21 NIV)

The Lord your God is with you, he is mighty to save. He will take great delight in you, he will quiet you with his love, he will rejoice over you with singing.
(Zephaniah 3:17 NIV)

Unless the LORD had helped me, I would soon have settled in the silence of the grave. I cried out, "I am slipping!" but your unfailing love, O LORD, supported me. When doubts filled my mind, your comfort gave me renewed hope and cheer. (Psalm 94:17-19 NLT)

33 It is God who arms me with strength and makes my way perfect. 17 "He reached down from on high and took hold of me; he drew me out of deep waters." 18 He rescued me from my powerful enemy, from my foes, who were too strong for me. 31 "As for God, his way is perfect; the word of the Lord is flawless. He is a shield for all who take refuge in him." (2 Samuel 22:33, 17, 18, 31 NIV)

The Lord gives strength to his people;
the Lord blesses his people with peace.
(Psalm 29:11 NIV)

As soon as I pray, you answer me; you encourage me by giving me strength. (Psalm 138:3 NLT)

A righteous man may have many troubles, but the Lord delivers him from them all; (Psalm 34:19 NIV)

"Then call on me when you are in trouble, and I will rescue you, and you will give me glory."
(Psalm 50:15 NLT)

Chapter 5

⚓ Resting with Jesus ⚓

Finding Peace

In the midst of our storms, we all long for peace. Fighting our storms on our own is exhausting, to say the least. We can only imagine the look on the Disciples' faces when, in the midst of the treacherous storm, they looked back to find Jesus asleep! We would all love to experience that type of peace in the midst of our storms of life.

According to Webster's dictionary, "peace" is said to mean "a state of tranquility, quiet, a state of security or freedom from disquieting or oppressive thoughts or emotions." As we grasp the message of "Jesus Calms the Storm," we can see why Jesus called out to the storm, "Peace!" It's exactly what the storm needed. It's exactly what we need too! Peace is what Jesus was experiencing in the back of the boat, and we desperately want to be with Jesus.

We wonder how anyone can have that much peace, especially under the circumstances. We wonder how we can ever have peace when we're living with an addict, when our family is falling apart from a rebellious teenager, when we lose our job and we have no way to support our family, when we face a terminal illness, when our depression is overcoming us, when we lose everything to an act of nature, when our nation is struck by terrorism, or when a loved one must go and fight a war. How can anyone have peace in the midst of such chaos? How could Jesus have a peace that surpasses our understanding?

The answer is simple: The peace that Jesus had can only come from faith in God . . . faith in God leads us *into His rest.* It's a place where peace resides *at all times . . . in all things.* When you enter into His rest . . .

Jesus calms the storm.

> *Jesus had peace in the back of the boat because He had entered into the rest of God.*
> *We, too, can enter into God's rest through our faith in Him.*
> *It's a place where peace resides at all times and in all things.*

Rest

The peace that Jesus had in the back of the boat wasn't by chance. He had entered into the rest of God. In the storms of our lives, we, too, must enter into the rest of God. And we can only enter in by our faith in Him. Here's the catch: The most important thing we must grasp about faith is that it involves both *ceasing* from our work *and making an effort.* It's coming to a place of saying, *"I can't do this — only God can."*

> It's the storm, all the pain and suffering, which creates the "turbulence" that motivates us to draw near to God and learn to depend upon Him through it all.

It's depending on God *for* everything . . . *in* everything. We instinctively rely on our own efforts and resources, instead of relying on the omniscient, omnipotent, and omnipresent power of God. Why is it that we think we're able to do God's job better than He can? Entering into the rest of God requires a deliberate choice to "let go and let God" . . . which is usually against our feelings and human wisdom.

As we struggle to step down off our throne and allow God to take His proper place in our life, we will see the clouds begin to part and a vision of light present a glimpse of why God has allowed the storm. The storm reveals a deeper need in our spirit. It reveals the discrepancy between *our* will and God's will for our lives. God is opening our eyes to see how desperately we need to depend upon His provision. The storm, all the pain and suffering, creates the "turbulence" which motivates us to draw near to Him; we learn to increasingly depend upon Him, while clinging to the Cross.

So there is a special rest still waiting for the people of God. For all who enter into God's rest will find rest from their labors, just as God rested after creating the world. Let us do our best to enter that place of rest.
(Hebrews 4:9-11 NLT)

As the storm rages, we're faced with our lack of faith; we suddenly realize that we must dig deeper into His Word. It's His Word that's the key to our faith, and it's our faith that brings us into His rest.

For the word of God is living and active. Sharper than any double-edged sword, it penetrates even to dividing soul and spirit, joints and marrow; it judges the thoughts and attitudes of the heart. (Hebrews 4:12 NIV)

While we're ceasing our struggling and relying on God's Promises, the Word goes to work within us; it takes root in our heart and points us to Jesus — the proper object of our faith. The storm on the Sea of Galilee pointed the Disciples to Jesus; God's purpose in *your* storm is to point you to Jesus, as well. It is through Jesus that we receive God's mercy and grace. *There is no other way.*

Jesus answered, "I am the way and the truth and the life. No one comes to the Father except through me."
(John 14:6 NIV)

It all comes down to surrender. And surrendering to a God whom we cannot see or hear challenges our intellect in an unprecedented way. It takes faith to surrender—*not human will or effort.* Although you may believe it takes an enormous amount of faith to believe in God, it actually takes far greater faith NOT to believe.

> *We have to cease leaning on our own understanding and start relying on the wisdom, strength, and power of our sovereign God.*

We have to cease leaning on our own understanding and start relying on the wisdom, strength, and power of our sovereign God.

So that your faith might not rest in the wisdom of men (human philosophy), but in the power of God.
(1 Corinthians 2:5 AMP)

To our own detriment, we usually rely on our own wisdom and lean upon our own understanding through our storms; we end up reasoning, struggling, and becoming constantly frustrated. By trusting in ourselves, we have no hope of entering into God's rest.

*Therefore, as the Holy Spirit says: Today, if you will hear His voice, Do not harden your hearts, as [happened] in the rebellion [of Israel] and their provocation and embitterment [of Me] in the day of testing in the wilderness, Where your fathers tried [My patience] and tested [My forbearance] and found I stood their test, and they saw My works for forty years. And so I was provoked (displeased and sorely grieved) with that generation, and said, They always err and are led astray in their hearts, and they have not perceived or recognized My ways and become progressively better and more experimentally and intimately acquainted with them. Accordingly, I swore in My wrath and indignation, **They shall not enter into My rest**.* (Hebrews 3:7-11 AMP)

We wrestle within . . . *we want to believe* . . . but how can we rest when the storm is raging? Our daily schedule leaves no time for "believing" — there is a job, kids, bills, and the consuming waves of hopelessness that comes with living in this fallen world. If only God would show Himself through "this storm." But, God doesn't work that way.

Testing him, they demanded that he show them a miraculous sign from heaven to prove his authority. When he

heard this, he sighed deeply in his spirit and said, "Why do these people keep demanding a miraculous sign? I tell you the truth, I will not give this generation any such sign." So he got back into the boat and left them.
(Mark 8:11-13 NLT)

He's given us His Word, embodied with countless miracles, which should give us *more than enough hope.* We believe by faith—not by proof. Jesus said, *"Because you have seen me, you have believed; blessed are those who have not seen and yet have believed"* (John 20:29 NIV). Faith believes God no matter what. It's trusting that God knows every detail of our circumstances; He has a plan . . . and *we can rest.*

> *We must realize that we can't change our circumstances . . . if the circumstances we're in are God's will.*

Releasing our hopes and dreams into the hands of God can be frightening. God's constant message of "Do not fear" continues to be the most powerful message to us through the storm. When we make the decision to turn our lives over into God's hands, fear overcomes us because we don't know what the outcome of our circumstances will be. The uncertainty haunts us because we're no longer in control. But, the truth is that when you allow God to take control . . . you are more in control of your life than ever before.

We must realize that we can't change our circumstances . . . if the circumstances we're in are God's will.

Don't allow yourself to be deceived, God's timing is perfect. He always shows up . . . just in time. It's just that, often times, He allows us to enter into a raging storm. He's teaching us how to enter into His rest. Entering into His rest is a deep spiritual need that is far greater than our need to be rescued out of the storm. If God instantly rescued us out of every storm of life, we'd miss the best part . . . *we'd miss a miracle!*

Just think what we would have been missed if Daniel had not been allowed to walk into the lion's den—we'd miss the miracle of God keeping the lion's mouths shut. If Shadrach, Meshach, and Abednego wouldn't have been thrown into the fiery furnace—we would have missed the miracle of them walking out without even the smell of smoke upon them! And what if Jesus would have gone to save Lazarus before he had died? Jesus wouldn't have had the opportunity to show Himself strong to those who were loyal to Him by raising Lazarus from the dead. God has shown us that He can do *all* things (close a den of lion's mouths), He is with us always (even *in* a fiery furnace), and His timing is perfect (Lazarus lived!). Every miracle in the Bible is a miracle for *you*. They all have a message, just as the miracle of "Jesus Calms the Storm" does.

Miracles come by trusting God; they come by faith and entering His rest. In learning how to have faith in God, there's one more thing we must learn to do.

If you aren't familiar with how to fish…then you need to learn. It's in your storms of life, when you're in the boat with Jesus, that you're going to need to learn to "cast."

Casting

Entering into God's rest is going to require some "casting." When we're casting in fishing, we're throwing the line *away* from us. "Cast," by Webster's definition, means "to shed, to throw forth, to turn, to direct, to drive out by force." Unfortunately, many of us try to cast our cares upon the Lord . . . and just as in fishing, we find that our cast has gotten our hook tangled in the trees behind us, snagged on the boat, or that we've hooked ourselves. These are *not* good casts; maybe you, like me, have been there . . . *spiritually and in fishing*!

> *A good "cast" doesn't get snagged*
> *on thoughts of doubt and fear.*
> *A good "cast" sheds the situation*
> *and turns it over to God;*
> *it's the success of our "cast"*
> *that reflects the quality of our faith.*

The success of our "cast" reflects the quality of our faith. We wonder if God truly cares, as our souls are "cast" into overwhelming despair. We feel as though God has "cast" us so far away from Him that He will never be able to hear us calling out through the raging storm. But, through the darkness, He brings light. Through the pain, we feel His hand reach for ours; through the roaring storm, we hear His voice whisper, *"Be Still."* And in that moment, though the fury of the storm refuses to cease, we know that *we are not alone.* God is ever faithful; He is with us always and nothing can separate us from Him.

For I am convinced that neither death nor life, neither angels nor demons, neither the present nor the future, nor any powers, neither height nor depth, nor anything else in all creation, will be able to separate us from the love of God that is in Christ Jesus our Lord. (Romans 8:38-39 NIV)

There is great reward for those who trust God. His *presence* is the biggest part of it. There is nothing that will calm the storm within you quicker than the assurance that the Almighty God, who parted the Red Sea, who made the blind see, who fed the five thousand with a few loaves of bread and fish, and who resurrected Christ, is ever–present in *your* life.

God's Promises give us all that we need to hold onto our faith in Him. When we maintain our unwavering confidence in the Lord, we find that *He is all we need*; He's the source of our strength. Don't cast away your confidence in God. He raised Lazarus from the dead with one word, "Rise!" He calmed the storm with one breath, "Peace! Be Still!"

God's hand is not so short that it cannot save, nor His ear so dull that He cannot hear (Isaiah 59:1).

Whether you see Him or not, He is at work in your life at this very moment. He specializes in turning the mundane into the meaningful and the ordinary into the extraordinary! You see, God not only moves in *unusual* and *unexpected* ways, He also moves on very *uneventful* days. The doors He closes in your life are just as much a part of His plan as the opened ones. He is just as magnificently involved in the mundane as He is in the miraculous. There comes a day, sometimes in a single moment, when mercy steps in and justice rolls down; God makes himself known in the most unimaginable ways. He often moves suddenly and powerfully—so take a step of faith and trust Him—*cast your faith upon Him.*

Therefore do not **cast** *away your confidence, which has great reward. For you have need of endurance, so that after you have done the will of God, you may receive the promise:* (Hebrews 10:35 NKJV)

So, what if we were to truly *cast* the situation we're struggling with at the moment? What if we drove our situation out from us by force? What if we said, *"Lord, this is now Your problem. You've told me to give it to You and now it's Yours. I will not worry over it for one more minute. I know that You are above all circumstances and if there is an answer, You have it, and You will solve it when You're ready. But right now, I can't live in peace and be burdened by this."* That's a really good cast! A "good" cast doesn't get snagged on thoughts of doubt and fear. What we come to realize is that when we truly "cast" our burden, we no longer struggle for answers. We don't fret about what the future will bring; we rest assured that God has it all handled.

As we wrestle with doubt, wondering if we can truly trust God when the storms wreak havoc in our lives . . . we can be certain through His Word that when He tells us to "cast," He's taking us deeper in our faith. When Jesus is in the boat with you, He will immerse your doubt and fear with His powerful presence and show you that with faith in Him . . . you'll experience miracles that will consume you with awe.

When he had finished speaking, he said to Simon, "Now go out where it is deeper, and let down your nets to catch some fish." "Master," Simon replied, "we worked hard all last night and didn't catch a thing. But if you say so, I'll let the nets down again." And this time their nets were so full of fish they began to tear! A shout for help brought their partners in the other boat, and soon both boats were filled with fish and on the verge of sinking. When Simon Peter realized what had happened, he fell to his knees before Jesus and said, "Oh, Lord, please leave me – I'm too much of a sinner to be around you." For he was awestruck by the number of fish they had caught, as were the others with him. (Luke 5:5-9 NLT)

It all comes down to "casting." It's all about being in a boat with Jesus and going deeper in your faith. And there's a technique you should know about that will help you to make "good casts": It's called *prayer*. In order to cast your burden to God, you have to pray. You must acknowledge to God that your situation is a disaster, it is destroying you, and you need His help. You must confess any sins that that are associated with your situation; ask God for His help in bringing you to a place of repentance, so that He can begin restoration.

Prayer will turn your focus away from your burdens and redirect it to God who can give you the guidance and strength that you will need to make it through the storm. The Scriptures, repeatedly, tell us to make our requests known to God. We're not to simply come to Him, but come to Him boldly, confidently.

So let us come boldly to the throne of our gracious God. There we will receive his mercy, and we will find grace to help us when we need it. (Hebrews 4:16 NLT)

> *Prayer turns your focus away from your burdens and redirects your soul to God, who can give you the guidance and strength that you need to make it through the storm.*

And we can be confident that he will listen to us whenever we ask him for anything in line with his will. And if we know he is listening when we make our requests, we can be sure that he will give us what we ask for.
(1 John 5:14-15 NLT)

You need to know that God hears you; but, He wants to see your confidence through your faith. He wants your heart to agree with what your mind knows. He wants you to understand that "His rest" is not a rest of weariness or inactivity, but of finished work. It's being confident that God has everything taken care of and you can go about your daily life experiencing peace. Faith in God, being at rest, is all about trusting in God and LIVING like you do!

Rising Above the Storm

As God takes you through the storm, He wants you to rise above it. When we're struggling with worry, disappointment, pain, and sorrow . . . we're *not* resting. We spend so much time worrying . . . there's obviously no time for rest. Psychology research has found that:

40% of worries are about events that will never happen.
30% of worries are about events that already happened.
22% of worries are about trivial events.
4% of worries are about events we cannot change.
4% of worries are about real events on which we can act.

So, the bottom line is, 96% of what we worry about . . . we have no control over! Even *Jesus* spoke of *worrying.*

And why do you worry about clothes? See how the lilies of the field grow. They do not labor or spin. Yet I tell you that not even Solomon in all his splendor was dressed like one of these. If that is how God clothes the grass of the field, which is here today and tomorrow is thrown into the fire, will he not much more clothe you, O you of little faith? So do not worry, saying, 'What shall we eat?' or 'What shall we drink?' or 'What shall we wear?' For the pagans run after all these things, and your heavenly Father knows that you need them. But seek first his kingdom and his righteousness, and all these things will be given to you as well. (Matthew 6:27-33 NIV)

We're *like* lilies of the field, except we tend to labor and spin! We are once again faced with being of "little faith." In times where our faith is failing, we're to seek God and fix our thoughts on things that are worthy of praise.

> *"His rest" is not a rest of weariness or inactivity, but of finished work.*
> *Faith in God, being at rest,*
> *is all about trusting in God*
> *and LIVING like you do!*

Fix your thoughts on what is true and honorable and right. Think about things that are pure and lovely and admirable. Think about things that are excellent and worthy of praise. (Philippians 4:8 NLT)

We *can* control our thoughts. God wouldn't ask us to do something that we aren't capable of doing; but, we're only able to be obedient to Him with His help . . . *in His strength*. If we can focus on the raging storm, then we can focus on God. It's just moving our mind in a different direction. And it's Jesus at rest in the storm that gets our attention! We can imagine the

moment when the Disciples turned to see Jesus
asleep. The heavy silence that consumed them was
probably enough to drown out the wind and waves
that were taking them under. That moment must
have seemed like eternity as they witnessed Jesus at
rest. That moment in time captured their attention
and capsized their pride. They needed a Savior to
save them . . . and *so do we*. He will take us *above* the
storm.

In all of creation, it's the eagles that can teach us
about rising above our storms in life.

But they that wait on the Lord shall renew their strength;
they shall mount up with wings like eagles;
they shall run, and not be weary;
and they shall walk and not faint.
(Isaiah 40:31 NIV)

From this simple Scripture, we learn a lot about
getting through storms. First, we understand that we
must *wait* upon the Lord. That means "being still!" If
we were "still," standing in faith and trusting in God,
we'd find a lot in common with the eagles because
we could prepare for the storm. You see, eagles know
a storm is coming long before it ever breaks. (If we
were more filled with God's Word, we'd know long
before a storm comes; many times, even prevent it by
avoiding it, overcoming it, or rising above it.) Once
the eagle anticipates the storm, he chooses a high
spot and waits for the winds to come. This is the key:
the eagle sets its wings so that when the wind ar-
rives, it will lift him high above the storm.

While the storm rages below, the eagle is soaring high above — gliding with ease. The eagle at no time ever tries to escape the storm, but rather looks for it, anticipates it, and finds its place above the storm. The eagle allows the storm to lift it up.

Humble yourselves, therefore, under God's mighty hand, that he may lift you up in due time. (1 Peter 5:6 NIV)

We can learn so much from this magnificent bird that God created and all humanity calls "majestic." We, too, should anticipate our storms. When we see them moving in, we should set our faith in God and let Him lift us up above the storm . . . where the eagles soar . . . the place where the eagle doesn't even concern itself with the wind's velocity or whether or not it changes direction. It's the place where the eagle is free from concern over how long the storm will last...the eagle is above it all. We, too, can rise above it all if we will allow God to lift us up; we rise above the storm by resting in the hands of God.

Lacking in Nothing

The faith it takes to rise above the storm, the faith that gives us peace through entering into the rest of God, takes persistence and patience. We don't just wake up one day, after deciding to have faith in God, and have the "patience" to endure and persevere through our storms of life. Patience comes from the Spirit as we rest our faith in God's hands.

What we come to realize is that although our internal storms can be calmed instantly, the external storm in this world will more than likely continue to rage. Only God knows the duration of our storms of life. Only He knows every intricate part of our lives; He designed us with purpose, and His plans will prevail— *whether or not we choose His way.*

O Lord, you have searched me and you know me. You know when I sit and when I rise; you perceive my thoughts from afar. You discern my going out and my lying down; you are familiar with all my ways. Before a word is on my tongue you know it completely, O Lord. You hem me in— behind and before; you have laid your hand upon me. Such knowledge is too wonderful for me, too lofty for me to attain. Where can I go from your Spirit? Where can I flee from your presence? If I go up to the heavens, you are there; if I make my bed in the depths, you are there. If I rise on the wings of the dawn, if I settle on the far side of the sea, even there your hand will guide me, your right hand will hold me fast. (Psalm 139:1-10 NIV)

We aren't born with patience . . . it's acquired through the Spirit; we're going to have to take steps through the journey to acquire it. Sometimes, the only way to develop patience is by going through a raging storm of life. Patience is part of resting in God. And although we're tempted to believe that we're to sit silently and simply "be patient . . ."it actually requires action. Deeper faith gives birth to patience. It is when we're "resting," clinging to our "Anchor,"

God's Word, that we find ourselves "lacking in nothing."

I have learned how to get along happily whether I have much or little. I know how to live on almost nothing or with everything. I have learned the secret of living in every situation, whether it is with a full stomach or empty, with plenty or little. (Philippians 4:11-12 NLT)

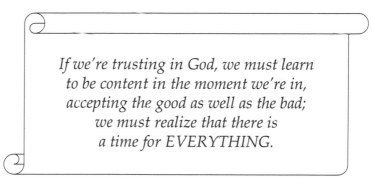

If we're trusting in God, we must learn to be content in the moment we're in, accepting the good as well as the bad; we must realize that there is a time for EVERYTHING.

We're going to have to rest, to wait, to be patient, because we are going to have to wait on God's timing. We will never be able to make something happen that only God can make happen. The Disciples weren't able to calm the storm on the Sea. All they could do was endure; often times, it's all we can do, too. But, as we endure, we can look toward the back of our boat and be reminded, Jesus is resting . . . and *so should we.*

You see, if God wants something to happen tomorrow, it will happen tomorrow. If He wants it to happen next year, it will happen next year. If he wants it to happen in the next half hour, well, you get the point. If God wants you to be married, He'll send you a mate. If God wants to give you a financial breakthrough, He'll inspire your boss to give you a promotion. If God wants you to be cured of a terminal disease, He can do that too.

But if He doesn't, or He doesn't do it in the timing you want Him to, then you're going to have to learn to wait. You're going to have to rest. You're going to have to trust Him while being content in the moment you're in.

> *Often times, all we can do is endure our storms of life. But, as we do, we can look in to the back of our boat and be reminded that Jesus is resting . . . and so should we.*

We must realize that there is a time for EVERY-THING. And *everything* means we must accept the good times as well as the bad; realizing that God permits them all . . . with greater purposes than we can often comprehend. There is a time for everything, and a season for every activity under heaven:

a time to be born and a time to die,
a time to plant and a time to uproot,

a time to kill and a time to heal,
a time to tear down and a time to build,

a time to weep and a time to laugh,
a time to mourn and a time to dance,

a time to scatter stones and a time to gather them,
a time to embrace and a time to refrain,

a time to search and a time to give up,
a time to keep and a time to throw away,

a time to tear and a time to mend,
a time to be silent and a time to speak,

a time to love and a time to hate,
a time for war and a time for peace.
(Ecclesiastes 3:1-8 NIV)

Don't give up on God. He has a *perfect* time for everything. He doesn't miss a thing . . . and He's well aware of the storm that rages in your life. God gives us more than enough hope through His Promises. And we must cling to His Promises because God usually doesn't reveal the exact timing of His plan ... He *mostly keeps us guessing.* Although it can be frustrating, the uncertainty keeps us focused upon Him. He knows that we might give up, if we knew how long it was going to take and what we'd have to go through to get to the mountaintop. He wants us to learn to embrace our time with Him in the *valley,* as well as the mountaintop; there's just as much joy there, and it makes the mountaintop so much more magnificent when we've had to travel so far to get there.

When God is directing our lives, when He's controlling the "seasons," we have to realize that we're just not going to be able to understand it all. We have to cease trying to figure it all out . . . *we'll never be able to anyway.*

A man's mind plans his way, but the Lord directs his steps and makes them sure. (Proverbs 16:9 AMP)

Man's steps are ordered by the Lord. How then can a man understand his way? (Proverbs 20:24 AMP)

Through these seasons of life, when storms break suddenly, we find that it is God who is breaking us. It's our brokenness . . . *it's surrendering* . . . that redirects our souls to the God who does the impossible. God uses our storms to prepare us for the incredible blessings He has planned for us—the "time" where we experience joy instead of pain.

God is at work. He wishes to accomplish something deep within us...things that will prepare us for storms of life that might otherwise destroy a less-obedient, less-committed, and less-prepared child of God. He's preparing us for greater things in life; but, in order to be a useful instrument of significance in the hands of God, we must be humbled and taught to trust Him. *He must break us . . . in order to bless us* (His ways are higher).

> *"It's doubtful that God can bless a man greatly*
> *until He has hurt him deeply."*
> — A.W. Tozer

In our times of desperation, when the season isn't yielding a harvest, there's only one way to come before God: with a humble heart. *He receives nothing else.* In fact, He sets himself against the proud. He says He opposes them, frustrates them, and defeats them. You see, there's a time to be broken, and there's a time to be made whole. And what you'll find is that your "brokenness "brings you much greater peace and joy than your "perceived" wholeness ever did.

God set Himself against the proud (the insolent, the over-bearing, the disdainful, the presumptuous, the boastful) – [and He opposes, frustrates, and defeats them], but gives grace (favor, blessing) to the humble. (1 Peter 5:5 AMP)

Our humble heart draws the help of God into our lives, in order to provide for our every need and protect us. He fully embraces the soul that cries out, *"God I don't know what to do, but I'm trusting in You."* God will allow the storms of our lives to bring us to the end of ourselves — to crucify our flesh, but never break our spirit. We can be certain that He will never allow a storm to rage for one moment more than is necessary to accomplish His purposes. He knows exactly what you can endure . . . and *it's much more than you think.*

*The temptations in your life are no different from
what others experience. And God is faithful.
He will not allow the temptation to be more
than you can stand. When you are tempted,
he will show you a way out so that you can endure.*
(1 Corinthians 10:13 NLT)

Each storm will bring with it a new way for us to shed our worldly nature and prove our faith to God. Why not believe that God can use your storms to make your life better than before? Why not take a step of faith and believe that He can do that? When the relentless waves are crashing down upon you, what have you got to lose? Here's a revelation: you have everything to lose if you don't trust . . . and everything to gain if you do.

"But anyone who hears my teaching and doesn't obey it is foolish, like a person who builds a house on sand. When the rains and floods come and the winds beat against that house, it will collapse with a mighty crash."
(Matthew 7:26-27 NLT)

When the storms of life come, and we've been promised that they will, you must make sure your house isn't built upon sand. Cling to the "Anchor" that is Jesus, the Living Word, and find your strength in Him. There is never a storm of life that is "calm." And although we may step out in faith and beg endlessly for God to calm the storm, *He simply may choose not to.* He may never change our circumstances, but *He will renew our strength and change our lives.* Your life may continue to be turbulent, seemingly unfair, filled with chaos, and agonizing pain; it may continue to fall apart at the seams. But, realize that many times, when your life is falling apart, *it's really just falling into place* in the hands of God.

> ## *The safest place to be is in the will of God.*
> — Anonymous

The next moment is as much beyond our grasp, and as much in God's care, as that a hundred years away. Care for the next minute is as foolish as care for a day in the next thousand years. In neither can we do anything, in both God is doing everything. — C.S. Lewis

Faith to Calm the Storm

God wants you to *completely* trust Him in this journey. He's taking you somewhere, and He's got work to do, in and through you, before you reach the destination. Know this, regardless of what kind of storm you're encountering . . . God is at work in it. He never ceases to work in a heart that is surrendered and focused upon Him. God has such grander purposes for our lives than we can ever imagine. His purposes are far greater than our health, prosperity, and seemingly "problem–free" lives. Our storms have a much higher purpose than for God to simply perform a miracle, in order to give us what we want, when we want it, in the way want it, and how we want it. Demanding *our way* in the storms of our lives would deprive us of far too many miracles that God desires to do.

God's goal in the storms is to develop our faith in Him for a greater goal of displaying His glory in and through our lives. It's in the storms of your life that you will learn to be at peace, content with whatever transpires, because you know you can take it from His loving hand. He will teach you to pray for what you want, surrender it all, and find joy in what He gives.

> *What you'll find is that your brokenness brings you much greater peace and joy than your "perceived" wholeness ever did.*

He'll show you that there's no room for you on His throne—*you belong at His feet.* You'll learn to stay focused on Him and continue to serve Him *in the midst of great uncertainty.* He'll open your heart to love others and care for their needs, *when your own heart is breaking.*

He'll strengthen you to live out your faith, *even when you can't see results;* you won't even see the clouds breaking. You'll learn the joy of being faithful, *even when your flesh wants to give up and run away.* It's through this amazing journey, where faith doesn't make things easy, *but makes all things possible* . . . God is at work, developing your faith, so that it will be more precious than gold. He wants you to have the faith that raises the dead to life, heals the sick, saves the lost, reconciles broken relationships, moves mountains, receives miracles in answer to prayer, calms the storms of your life, and *rests in Him alone.*

When you struggle to understand it all, you'll find that although God may not calm the storm, He'll calm *you.* In the lyrics of Scott Krippayne's song, *"Sometimes He Calms the Storm,"* we find, once again, that God has given us an "Anchor," which is Christ, who gives us all that we need to weather the storm, as we sail the *sea of faith.*

All who sail the sea of faith
Find out before too long
How quickly blue skies can grow dark
And gentle winds grow strong
Suddenly fear is like white water
Pounding on the soul
Still we sail knowing
That our Lord is in control

Sometimes He calms the storm
With a whispered peace **be still**
He can settle any sea
But it doesn't mean He will
Sometimes He holds us close
And lets the wind and waves go wild
Sometimes He calms the storm
And other times He calms His child

He has a reason for each trial
That we pass through in life
And though we're shaken
We cannot be pulled apart from Christ
No matter how the driving rain beats down
On those who hold to faith
A heart of trust will always
Be a quiet peaceful place

The rest of God, His peace, can only be experienced through completely trusting in Him. And we know that trusting in God can only come from relying upon His Promises. As we take each step of faith, we will find that God is faithful to His Word. When we experience His faithfulness, our faith grows and we are eager to take another step. He's drawing us nearer. He's extending an invitation to take a journey with Him. (Trust me, take Him upon it . . . you won't regret it!)

> *In the storms of your life, you will learn to be content with whatever transpires because you can take it from God's loving hand. He will teach you to pray for what you want, surrender it all, and find joy in what He gives.*

He wants to show you that when you apply the Word to your life, you will find yourself filled with confident hope in the most undesirable and over-whelming circumstances. When you listen to what God has to say to you through His Word and when you apply it to your life, you'll find that you have faith that calms the storm.

All Scripture is inspired by God and is useful to teach us what is true and to make us realize what is wrong in our lives. It straightens us out and teaches us to do what is right. It is God's way of preparing us in every way, fully equipped for every good thing God wants us to do.
(2 Timothy 3:16-17 NLT)

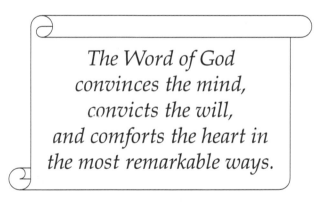

The Word of God convinces the mind, convicts the will, and comforts the heart in the most remarkable ways.

It's through His Word that you can walk confi-dently in faith that the One who holds the world in His hands is *holding you*. Instead of becoming over-whelmed by your storms, you learn with each step of faith that you can gain the faith and peace that Jesus had in the back of the boat. *"Being Still"* becomes a vital part of your walk with God because storms of life are inevitable; yet we have Jesus, our "Anchor," who is immovable. His Word is a miracle, in and of itself. The Word of God speaks to every part of who we are. It convinces the mind, convicts the will, and comforts the heart in the most remarkable ways. The most powerful miracle in your life will be when you make the choice to make the Bible your map for life.

Let God navigate . . . *He's much more capable of seeing what lies ahead in your journey.* He is the ultimate GPS (Global Positioning System)! His Word will take you on a journey that will permeate every aspect of your life. Immersing yourself in the Word of God will give you extraordinary strength, fill you with amazing peace, and bring about great calming in *all* of your storms of life.

For every child of God defeats this evil world by trusting Christ to give the victory. And the ones who win this battle against the world are the ones who believe that Jesus is the Son of God. (1 John 5:4-5 NLT)

The question is, "Is Jesus with *you* in *your* boat?" If He is, if you see Him, if you believe He is there, are you living your life in the storm as if He is? We're told to examine our faith to see if it is genuine.

Examine and test and evaluate your own selves to see whether you are holding to your faith and showing the proper fruits of it. Test and prove yourselves [not Christ]. Do you not yourselves realize and know [thoroughly by an ever-increasing experience] that Jesus Christ is in you — unless you are [counterfeits] disapproved on trial and rejected? (2 Corinthians 13:5 AMP)

Do you have the faith that reaches out for the hand of God even when you're blinded by the wind and waves of the storm? Do you act upon your faith in God by taking every thought captive and asking God to speak to you through His Word? Have you resigned your life into God's hands? Are you relying on Him to show you the direction and attitude to take in your storm? Do you humbly and thankfully accept the storms of your life as being permitted by His loving hand? Do you give praise in the storm, regardless of whether or not you can see the storm clouds breaking? Is your heart set to wait on Him, regardless of how long it takes? Do you continue to trust God even when everything in the natural seems to contradict the faith you cling to? Is your Spirit at rest in the most turbulent storms in your life? Have you surrendered all your doubts and fears to Him? Are you focused upon how great your problem is instead of how great your God is? Do you truly believe that God will work a miracle for you that you cannot conceive? Do you recognize when Jesus is beside you or do you look right past Him? You see, for all the questions we have for God . . . *He's has questions for us too.*

> *For all the questions*
> *we have for God . . .*
> *He has questions for us, too.*

Don't allow the lies of the enemy to deceive you; *you can't save yourself* . . . you never could . . . and you'll never be able to. *Only Jesus saves.* So, when you're crying out to God for a miracle because your boat is capsizing in the storm, you will find Jesus awaking from His rest, turning to you and asking, *"Where is your faith?"* You will only experience a magnificent miracle and the calming of your storms in life if you will *"Be Still,"* and have faith in the *One* who controls them.

May God bless you always through His Word.
If you should ever need Scripture, God's Promises,
for any circumstance in your life, please visit:

http://www.ScriptureNow.com

or email:
godsword@scripturenow.com

Scriptures to Encourage You in the Storm

Be Still, and know that I am God! (Psalm 46:10 NLT)

But I have stilled and quieted my soul;
(Psalm 131:2 NIV)

Meditate in your heart upon your bed, and be still.
(Psalm 4:4 NASB)

In the day of my trouble I will call on You,
for You will answer me. (Psalm 86:7 AMP)

When he arrived and saw what grace (favor) God was bestowing upon them, he was full of joy; and he continuously exhorted (warned, urged, and encouraged) them all to cleave unto and remain faithful to and devoted to the Lord with [resolute and steady] purpose of heart.
(Acts 11:23 AMP)

Do not let your hearts be troubled (distressed, agitated). You believe in and adhere to and trust in and rely on God; believe in and adhere to and trust in and rely also on Me.
(John 14:1 AMP)

God is our refuge and strength, always ready to help in times of trouble. (Psalm 46:1 NLT)

And so, Lord, where do I put my hope?
My only hope is in you. (Psalm 39:7 NLT)

Now may our Lord Jesus Christ himself and God our Father, who loved us and by his grace gave us eternal comfort and a wonderful hope, comfort you and strengthen you in every good thing you do and say.
(2 Thessalonians 2:16-17 NLT)

I say to myself, "The LORD is my inheritance; therefore, I will hope in him!" (Lamentations 3:24 NLT)

But I will hope continually, and will praise You yet more and more.
(Psalm 71:14 AMP)

To them God has chosen to make known among the Gentiles the glorious riches of this mystery, which is Christ in you, the hope of glory. (Colossians 1:27 NIV)

May the God of hope fill you with all joy and peace as you trust in him, so that you may overflow with hope by the power of the Holy Spirit. (Romans 15:13 NIV)

Let us hold unswervingly to the hope we profess, for he who promised is faithful. (Hebrews 10:23 NIV)

But as for me, I watch in hope for the LORD, I wait for God my Savior; my God will hear me. (Micah 7:7 NIV)

I will praise you forever for what you have done; in your name I will hope, for your name is good.
(Psalm 52:9 NIV)

. . . in order that we, who were the first to hope in Christ, might be for the praise of his glory. (Ephesians 1:12 NIV)

No one whose hope is in you will ever be put to shame. (Psalm 25:3 NIV)

We want each of you to show this same diligence to the very end, in order to make your hope sure. (Hebrews 6:11 NIV)

For who is God besides the LORD? And who is the Rock except our God? It is God who arms me with strength and makes my way perfect. (Psalm 18:31-32 NIV)

He gives strength to the weary and increases the power of the weak. (Isaiah 40:29 NIV)

You are my hiding place; you will protect me from trouble and surround me with songs of deliverance. (Psalm 32:7 NIV)

The Lord is my rock and my fortress and my deliverer; (2 Samuel 22:2 NKJV)

May the God of hope fill you with all joy and peace as you trust in him, so that you may overflow with hope by the power of the Holy Spirit. (Romans 15:13 NIV)

God's Word On . . .

Anger

Psalm 37:8
Psalm 103:8
Proverbs 14:29
Proverbs 15:1
Proverbs 15:18
Proverbs 19:11
Ecclesiastes 7:9
Ephesians 4:26
Ephesians 4:31, 32
Colossians 3:8
James 1:19,20

Anxiety

Deuteronomy 31:6
Psalm 86:7
Psalm 139: 23, 24
Matthew 6:27
Matthew 6:31, 33
Matthew 6:34
Mark 4:19
Philippians 4:6, 7

Bitterness

Matthew 5:43-48
Matthew 6:12, 14-15
Mark 11:25
John 8:7
Romans 12:19
Colossians 3:12-15
Philippians 3:13-15
Hebrews 8:12
Hebrews 12:15

Confessing the Word

Psalm 119:105
Isaiah 48:6, 7
Jeremiah 1:12
Romans 4:17
Hebrews 4:12
Hebrews 10:23

Confidence

Joshua 1:9
Psalm 18:29
Psalm 37:3
Psalm 57:7
Psalm 84:12
Psalm 131: 1, 2
Proverbs 29:25
Isaiah 26:3
Isaiah 30:15
Micah 7:7
Philippians 1:6
Philippians 3:3
Hebrews 4:16
Hebrews 10:35

Consequences

Psalm 40:12
Proverbs 13:5
Isaiah 59:2
Jeremiah 6:15
Romans 6:23
Titus 1:15
Revelation 20; 14, 15

Contentment

Psalm 16:6
Psalm 17:15
Psalm 84:10
Psalm 107:8, 9
Proverbs 14:30
John 6:35
Philippians 4:10, 11
Philippians 4:19
1 Timothy 6:6, 8
Hebrews 13:5, 6

Depression

Deuteronomy 31:8
Psalm 3:3
Psalm 34:15, 17
Psalm 40: 1-3
Psalm 42:5
Psalm 42: 6, 8, 11
Psalm 77: 1, 2
Psalm 91:14-16
Isaiah 54:4
Isaiah 60:1
1 Peter 5:6, 7

Discouragement

Psalm 3:3
Psalm 30:11, 12
John 10:10
John 16:33
Romans 8:28
2 Corinthians 1:4
2 Corinthians 4:8
2 Corinthians 4:16, 17
2 Corinthians 12:9
Philippians 4:13

Encouragement/ Comfort

Psalm 27:5
Psalm 31:7
Psalm 57:2, 3
Psalm 62:1, 2
Psalm 119:50
Psalm 138:7, 8
2 Corinthians 1:3, 4
2 Corinthians 4:17, 18
2 Thessalonians 2:16

Faith

Habakkuk 2:4
Matthew 17:20
Mark 11:23
Romans 3:28
Romans 5:2
Romans 10:17
Romans 14:23
Romans 15:13
1 Corinthians 2:5
2 Corinthians 5:7
Galatians 3:24, 25
Ephesians 3:12
1 Timothy 6:12
Hebrews 10:22, 23
Hebrews 11:1, 3
Hebrews 11:6
James 2:17

Fear

Psalm 23:4
Psalm 27:1
Psalm 91:4, 5
Psalm 112:7, 8
Proverbs 29:25
Isaiah 41:10
Isaiah 54:14
Luke 12:32
2 Timothy 1:7
Hebrews 13:5, 6
1 Peter 3:14
1 John 4:18

Forgiveness

2 Chronicles 30:9
Psalm 51:7, 9
Matthew 6:14
Isaiah 53:5
Mark 11: 25, 26
Romans 3:11, 12, 21, 22
Luke 6:37
Romans 8:10, 12
Romans 4:7, 8
2 Corinthians 5:21
Ephesians 4:32
Hebrews 1:3

Grace

Psalm 84:11
Acts 13:43
Romans 3:24
Romans 5:15
Romans 5:20, 21
1 Corinthians 3:9-11
Ephesians 2:8
James 4:6

Guilt and Condemnation

Psalm 18:23
Psalm 51:1, 2
Colossians 3:13
Hebrews 10:22, 23
James 5:15
1 John 3:18-20
1 John 1:9, 10
1 John 2:12

Health and Healing

Psalm 30:2
Psalm 103:2, 3
Psalm 107:20
Psalm 118:17
Psalm 147:3
Proverbs 4:20-22
Isaiah 58:8
Jeremiah 17:14
Jeremiah 30:17
James 5:14, 15
1 Peter 2:24

Hope

Psalm 33:18
Psalm 147:11
Proverbs 13:12
Lamentations 3:24-26
Romans 12:12
Romans 15:4
Romans 15:13
Ephesians 1:18
1 Peter 1:13

Hearing from God

Deuteronomy 28:1
Psalm 40:6
Psalm 95:7, 8
Jeremiah 7:23
Jeremiah 33:3
Matthew 7:24, 25
Matthew 13:19, 23
John 10:27
Romans 10:17
James 1:22-25

Humility and Pride

Psalm 25:9
Psalm 69:32
Psalm 147:6
Proverbs 11:2
Proverbs 15:33
Proverbs 16:19
Proverbs 29:23
Micah 6:8
James 4:10
1 Peter 5:6

Loneliness

Genesis 28:15
1 Samuel 12:22
Psalm 25:16
Psalm 27:10
Psalm 46:1
Isaiah 41:10
Matthew 28:20
John 14:18
2 Corinthians 6:18
Hebrews 13:5

Patience

Psalm 37:34
Psalm 40:1
Ecclesiastes 7:8
Romans 5:3, 4
Galatians 6:9
Colossians 1:11, 12
Hebrews 6:11, 12
James 1:2-4
James 5:7, 8
Revelation 3:10

Peace

Job 22:21
Proverbs 16:7
Isaiah 26:3
Isaiah 54:10
John 14:27
Philippians 4:7
2 Thessalonians 3:16
Hebrews 12:14

Prayer

Job 22:27
Psalm 34:4, 15
Psalm 38:15
Psalm 145:18, 19
Proverbs 15:29
Isaiah 55:6
Matthew 7:7, 8
Matthew 18:19
Luke 18:1
John 16:24
Romans 8:26
1 Thessalonians 5:17
Hebrews 4:16

Protection

Deuteronomy 33:27
Job 11:18, 19
Psalm 9:9
Psalm 32:7
Psalm 91: 1, 2
Psalm 91: 9-11
Proverbs 14:26

Receiving God's Love

Proverbs 8:17
John 3:16
John 15:9
John 16:27
Romans 5:5
1 Corinthians 8:3
1 Corinthians 16:14
2 Corinthians 5:14, 15
Ephesians 3:17-19
Ephesians 4:15
Ephesians 5:2
1 John 4:16
1 John 4:19
Jude 20, 21

Seeking God

Deuteronomy 4:29
2 Chronicles 7:14
2 Chronicles 15:2
Psalm 27:4
Lamentations 3:25
Matthew 6:33
Matthew 7:7, 8
John 5:30
Colossians 3:1
Hebrews 11:6

Self-Control

Proverbs 15:18
Proverbs 25:28
Ecclesiastes 5:2
Ecclesiastes 7:9
Lamentations 3:26, 27
Luke 21:19
1 Corinthians 6:12
1 Corinthians 13: 4, 5
Galatians 5:22, 23
Colossians 3:12-14
2 Peter 1:5-7

Selfishness

Proverbs 28:27
Mark 8:34
Romans 12:10
Romans 15:2
1 Corinthians 9:19
1 Corinthians 10:24
1 Corinthians 10:33
2 Corinthians 5:15
Galatians 6:2
Philippians 2:3-7
1 Timothy 5:6
1 John 3:17, 18

Spiritual Warfare

Deuteronomy 28:7
Psalm 35:1-3
Romans 7:23-25
Romans 8:37
2 Corinthians 10:3, 4
Ephesians 6:11
1 Timothy 6:12
1 Peter 2:11, 12
1 Peter 5:8

Stress

Psalm 37:5
Psalm 39:6
Isaiah 40:29
Matthew 6:25, 31, 33
Mark 4:19
Luke 12:27
Luke 21:34
1 Corinthians 7:32
Philippians 4:6
Philippians 4:8, 9
1 Peter 5:7

Trust

Psalm 18:2, 3
Psalm 20:7
Psalm 31:14, 15
Psalm 56:3, 4
Psalm 62:8
Proverbs 3:5-8
Proverbs 29:25
Isaiah 30:15
Nahum 1:7
Hebrews 2:13

Victory

2 Samuel 8:6
1 Chronicles 29:11
Psalm 149:4
Proverbs 24:6
Romans 8:37
1 Corinthians 15:54, 57
2 Corinthians 2:14
1 John 5:1-5

Waiting on God

Psalm 25:5
Psalm 31:14, 15
Psalm 37:7
Psalm 39:7, 8
Psalm 62:1, 2
Psalm 145:15, 16
Isaiah 30:18
Isaiah 40:31
Habakkuk 2:3

Wisdom

Psalm 111:10
Proverbs 1:5
Proverbs 2:1-5
Proverbs 3:5-7
Proverbs 3:13-15
Proverbs 3:35
Proverbs 8:11
Proverbs 8:35
Proverbs 19:20
James 1:5

Worry

Psalm 27:1
Psalm 46:1
Psalm 91:9, 10
Psalm 112: 7
Proverbs 1:33
Isaiah 26:3
Isaiah 43:2
Isaiah 54:4
Matthew 6:27
Matthew 6:31, 34
Mark 4:40
John 16:33
Romans 8:28
Philippians 4:6, 7

About the Author

*Cherie Hill is the founder of ScriptureNow.com
Ministry which brings the Word of God
into over 30 countries around the world.
She has a BA in Psychology and is trained in
Biblical Counseling through the AACC.
She is a Bestselling Christian Living author,
ranked in the top 10 authors for Religion and Spirituality,
who spends her time at the feet of Jesus.*

Author of:

WAITING on GOD

Hope Being Gone

BE STILL
(Let Jesus Calm Your Storms)

Beginning at The End
(Finding God When Your World Falls Apart)

THE WAYS of GOD
(Finding Purpose Through Your Pain)

empty.
(Living Full of Faith When Life Drains You Dry)

Made in the USA
Lexington, KY
17 March 2016